Fighting
Depression

Keats Titles of Related Interest

Nutritional Influences on • Melvyn R. Werbach, M.D.
Illness

The Nutrition Desk • Robert H. Garrison, Jr.,
Reference M.A., R.Ph. and Elizabeth
Somer, M.A., R.D.

Wellness Medicine • Robert A. Anderson, M.D.

Dr. Wright's Guide to • Jonathan V. Wright, M.D.
Healing with Nutrition

Diet and Disease • E. Cheraskin, M.D., D.M.D.,
W.M. Ringsdorf, Jr., D.M.D.
and J. W. Clark, D.D.S.

Brain Allergies • William H. Philpott, M.D.
and Dwight K. Kalita, Ph.D.

Common Questions on • Abram Hoffer, M.D., Ph.D.
Schizophrenia and their
Answers

Orthomolecular Medicine • Abram Hoffer, M.D., Ph.D.
for Physicians

The Healing Nutrients • Eric R. Braverman, M.D.
Within with Carl C. Pfeiffer, M.D.,
Ph.D.

Fighting Depression

Harvey M. Ross, M.D.

Keats Publishing, Inc.  New Canaan, Connecticut

Fighting Depression is not intended as medical advice. Its intent is solely informational and educational. Please consult a health professional should the need for one be indicated.

FIGHTING DEPRESSION

Library of Congress Cataloging-in-Publication Data

Ross, Harvey M.
    Fighting depression / Harvey M. Ross.—2nd rev. ed.
        p.   cm.
    Includes index.
    ISBN 0-87983-582-6 : $9.95
    1. Depression, Mental—Treatment. 2. Depression, Mental—
Etiology. 3. Hypoglycemia—Popular works.—I. Title.
    [DNLM: 1. Depressive Disorder—therapy. WM 171 E824f]
RC537.R65   1992
616.85'270654—dc20
DNLM/DLC
for Library of Congress   92-15456
                                                        CIP

Printed in the United States of America

Published by Keats Publishing, Inc.
27 Pine Street (Box 876)
New Canaan, Connecticut 06840-0876

*To my Mother and Father, who
by their love, guidance and
support, have made possible
for their children
all that is worthwhile.*

Acknowledgment Is Given with Gratitude:

To Jacqueline Zimmermann, who conceived this book and whose encouragement kept me working happily.
To Frank Murray for his interest and expert editorial assistance.
To my patients, who continue to teach me by sharing their thoughts, observations and experiences.
To Ronald L. Platt, whose counsel has never failed and who has led to exciting areas which otherwise would not have been.
To Allan and Janet Cott, who years ago gave their friendship and introduced me to orthomolecular psychiatry, which has brought me the greatest reward of pleasure in my work.

HARVEY M. ROSS, M.D.

Contents

CONTENTS

Preface

WHEN I WAS in medical school at Emory University in Atlanta, Georgia, there was a marvelous Professor of Medicine whose name I don't remember but whose wisdom, kindness, intelligence and compassion I will never forget. It was not his teaching of the rare diseases that I remember, but, rather, his approach to the needs of patients. He was a good listener. And he stressed the insight of patients and the wisdom that a person has about his own body, a wisdom that has nothing to do with intelligence or education.

"If a patient comes to you with a headache and complains that there are little men with hammers pounding away inside his head, it's your job to look for the little men!" he would say.

After medical school and psychiatric training in New York City, I became a staff psychiatrist at a 200-bed hospital that was predominantly psychiatric. Gracie Square Hospital is in Manhattan and the patients suffered from an array of psychiatric disorders. But the reason for their admission was generally uncontrolled schizophrenia or severe depression. The average stay in the hospital was under three weeks. Treatment was active and vigorous. It was here that I became involved in many treatments, such as convulsive treatments and pharmacotherapy. Later I became interested in orthomolecular psychiatry and regularly use megavitamin therapy and a corrective diet to deal with depression and other mental disorders.

Gracie Square Hospital has over 1,000 psychiatrists on its visiting staff. About 100 of the physicians use the hospital facilities for their private patients. Lothar Kalinowsky and David Impastato, both well known for their expertise in convulsive therapy; Nathan Kline, known for his accomplishments in therapy with medications—especially anti-depressants—frequently admitted their patients.

During those early years as a staff psychiatrist, I also did private practice, which was a composite of analytic orientation, support, dealing with the here and now, and directive therapies. The physical therapies were also used. Although I was intellectually pleased with the insights that my patients would develop, I was often disappointed by the lack of improvement that I thought should follow those insights. Since then I have reasoned that the therapy was not at fault; it was my error in employing a valuable tool incorrectly: It was like using tweezers to weed your garden. Tweezers are a very useful instrument—if used for the purpose for which they are intended.

It was in this setting that I began to give electro-convulsive treatments to the patients of Dr. Allan Cott, a megavitamin therapist. In the treatment of severely schizophrenic patients who have not shown a response to vitamins and tranquilizers, electro-convulsive treatment may be prescribed. At first, without any clinical investigation, I thought that the use of vitamins was a harmless gimmick. I saw the patients getting well, but I assumed that it was mainly because of the electro-convulsive treatment. However, I did have a vague impression that the patients on megavitamins responded more rapidly to electroconvulsive treatments and were left with less undesirable side effects than my other patients who were not on vitamins. I became more convinced of the efficacy of megavitamin therapy when Dr. Cott asked me to take his emergency calls for three weeks while he was away.

I received three or four telephone calls from patients' families, who reported that, within 24 to 48 hours after the patient willfully stopped the vitamins or suggested diet, many schizophrenic symptoms returned. I remained skeptical but at least my interest was aroused. For the next several months, I began to observe Dr. Cott's patients closely. Then I tried his method with several of my own patients whom I had treated for years with very little change, in spite of psychotherapy, medication and, in one case, frequent hospitalizations and shock treatments.

As I began to notice encouraging changes in some of my patients—who had shown no changes for years—I recognized megavitamin therapy as a valid therapy. The following three years proved to be busy, happy, interesting and professionally satisfying. While sharing an office with Dr. Allan Cott, I was able to learn more about megavitamin therapy from Allan and his well-informed wife, Janet. Even though I moved to California in 1972, these consultations still go on.

In the following chapters, I will tell you more about depression and how I treat it. Although I will be devoting a great deal of attention to orthomolecular psychiatry, I do wish to say that this is by no means the only treatment available. The more stubborn cases of depression require various approaches because, after all, the most important thing is to cure the patient of his depression. But I do believe that nutritional therapy is unjustifiably ignored by many doctors and psychiatrists, and that it offers hope and improvement to the countless millions who are suffering from a variety of psychiatric disorders.

I wish to emphasize—and this is the leitmotif of this book—that there is so much medical, psychiatric and nutritional help available that no one should ever stay depressed. There are also so many competent professionals in this field that help is almost as near as your telephone. Don't let another day pass before taking positive steps to rid yourself or a loved one from the frightening, debilitating illness known as depression.

Preface to Revised Edition

OVER TEN YEARS have passed since I sat down in the cool summer air in Aspen to start writing *Fighting Depression*. The description of depression given then is as valid now: people continue to suffer from depression now as then; suicides in depressed people continue now as then; but, happily, more is being done now to treat depression.

More is being done because more has been learned about conditions which contribute to the causes of some depressions; the more specific the cause, the more specific the treatment. For example, the prescription of the proper antibiotic for a bacterial infection, once the bacteria has been identified, has a better chance of being effective than the advice to take two aspirin and drink warm liquids. Depressions which have been resistant to treatment have been showing improvement in many cases, where new causes of depressions are considered and found to be present.

The areas of therapy which have occupied a significant amount of my professional time and are discussed in this revised edition are food sensitivities and Candida (yeast) sensitivity. Both of these conditions are manifested by depression in addition to other symptoms.

Also of importance is the recognition depression may be one of the major symptoms of chronic viral infections.

FIGHTING DEPRESSION

Precursor therapy, the use of amino acids to influence the production of neurotransmitters, is a promising and exciting addition to the therapeutic tools available for treatment of depression.

Further discussion of the hypoglycemic diet is found in this revision. I have also included many questions about hypoglycemia which I have heard very often from my patients.

These new treatments and conditions, which are recognized by many as contributors to depression, have not yet eradicated depression, but as signs of the continued attack on depression they give new hope to the depressed person.

HARVEY M. ROSS, M.D.
Hollywood, California
March, 1987

Preface to Second Revision

In the sixteen years since *Fighting Depression* was first printed there has not been a lessening of the incidence of depression in the population, nor of the suffering it causes to those with the disease and to their family and friends, but there is a greater acceptance of the concept that depression is not always caused by life's events. Psychiatric journals are now filled with the effect or lack of effect of new medications; month after month articles describe basic research into the biochemical nature of depression. However, the most common nutritional and other medical causes of depression are still largely ignored or dismissed as unimportant by the medical profession.

Fighting Depression starts where most discussions of causes of depression stop. Hypoglycemia, food sensitivities, yeast sensitivities and viral diseases are discussed in order to point out some common medical/nutritional causes of depression which are frequently overlooked in the doctors' offices. Old and new therapies are outlined in separate chapters. And finally, suggestions are made on how to obtain help, with some of the causes and therapies revealed in *Fighting Depression*.

This revision could not have been done without the ongoing help of Christine Coueron, who keeps my office running, and Barbra Ross and Jean Trousdale, who keep me running.

Harvey M. Ross, M.D.

Hollywood, California
August, 1991

xvii

PART 1

Understanding Depression

CHAPTER 1

Depression May Afflict Anyone

A LARGE PSYCHIATRIC clinic in the Midwest recently found that, of 5,000 patients referred for outpatient care, about one-third had depression. Sometimes depression is the patient's only complaint; at other times it is only part of the overall problem. But depression is a complaint that the average psychiatrist deals with in a high percentage of his patients. It is a traumatic experience because it disrupts family life and may result in suicide, the ultimate danger for the depressed person.

Like many life occurrences, depression is defined in the eyes of the beholder. And like three blind men, who each described an elephant differently, depression is seen and understood differently by the patient, the family and the physician. The patient is the one who shows the sadness, withdrawn behavior, tearfulness, hopelessness, loss of self esteem and self abuse that can be recognized as prominent symptoms of the illness. People close to the depressed person have another view. If the condition is recognized as a disease, then the family is in a better position to be helpful and lighten the burden. Too frequently the family refuses to recognize the depression as an illness, and they either offer poor advice or treat the patient with contempt.

3

UNDERSTANDING DEPRESSION

This attack on the depressed person only serves to confirm his sense of worthlessness. The third important view of depression comes from the physician. He is not only interested in recognizing the disease, but also in making a more specific diagnosis of the illness so that proper treatment may be started. Obviously different types of depression require different treatments. Treatments may vary from the purely nutritional to the purely psychological. There are many situations where a combination of treatments is necessary for the maximum results.

After a preliminary examination, the physician must make a diagnosis. This is done by talking to the patient and also anyone who is close to the patient. During the information gathering period, the physician–psychiatrist observes the mood, behavior and thinking of the patient. Physical examination, psychological testing and laboratory examinations are all part of the routine After all of the information has been obtained, the physician should have enough material to make his diagnosis and to outline a treatment plan.

When the family or patient is confronted with the suggested treatment, some confusion may arise. Hopefully, some of the confusion of psychiatric treatments for depression will be lessened by this book. The more common treatments, not necessarily in the order of prominence are: orthomolecular psychiatry (megavitamin therapy), psychotherapy, medication, shock treatment and the use of lithium, a trace mineral.

In his practice, the average physician–psychiatrist sees a wide spectrum of depression cases. Fortunately, many of the patients are returned to a normal life. For others it would be almost impossible to second-guess that they were bent on self-destruction. Here are some typical cases showing the diversity of depression.

• At 5 a.m., a middle-aged woman climbed to the roof of a five-story apartment building and jumped off, killing herself instantly.

4

DEPRESSION MAY AFFLICT ANYONE

• A young man in his twenties left a note for his family and walked off into the mountainous woods to die under a tree.

• Chris, a bright, red-haired, freckled, eleven-year-old boy, cried every time his parents talked to him.

• Frank, a hard-working, previously aggressive contractor, caught in a combination of bad deals and bad times and seeing his hard-earned fortune on the verge of collapse, finds himself unable to cope with day-to-day decisions.

• Following the birth of her baby, a young mother won't do anything but stay in bed and cry.

• For the past ten years, Lorrie, a usually happy mother and wife of a successful businessman, has learned to give up three months of her life every Spring because she is unable to take care of her usual chores while she withdraws from her family, friends and volunteer work.

All of these people are victims of depression, that disturbance of mood which leaves a person sad. But we've all been sad without being depressed. Watching the heroine lose the hero might make some people sad. Graduating from high school or college and moving on to the next step in life may be accompanied by sadness. Seeing a loved one depart for a week or a year usually provokes sadness. Watching your team lose in the World Series may trigger a temporary melancholia.

But with clinical depression there is much more than sadness; there is a degree of hopelessness. A depressed person is likely to see his state of affairs as permanent. There is the feeling that life will never be anything but sad. There seems to be no hope for the future.

Varying degrees of hopelessness are present. Some depressed people recognize their hopelessness as an emotional quality, while their intellect tells them otherwise; they feel that their hopelessness is a product of their illness. These people have some insight into the illness. Others are not as fortunate; both their head and their heart tell them that their case is hopeless.

5

UNDERSTANDING DEPRESSION

The determination of the heart and head aspects of the individual's depression is an important factor the doctor uses in planning the treatment. Depressions can vary in severity, depending on the head and heart factors of hopelessness. The most severe depression, of course, is when the person is convinced in his heart and head that there is no hope for him. The severe depression represents a true psychiatric emergency because it is in this group that suicides present the greatest risk.

It is easy to understand when a person has given up all hope of ever being anything but depressed and is sentenced to a life of sadness with no joy that he may seek suicide as a solution. The emotional pain of depression is intense. The least severe depression is characterized by a hopeless feeling that comes and goes but is always recognized by the head as being a symptom of illness and not reality. Between these two extremes one finds an infinite variety of depressions.

The feelings of sadness and hopelessness show many outward signs. The sadness is noticeable by a lack of a sense of humor. Everything becomes heavy, overpowering and gloomy. Normally sad events are exaggerated. Other events are either ignored or distorted to become sad. Nowhere can a thread of joy be found. Every situation is recognized only for its damaging aspects.

The depressed person does not go out of his way to find the negative aspects in his life. His thinking is as natural as if he were wearing magic glasses that exaggerated all the negative qualities of every event and eliminated anything positive. Besides the obvious signs of sadness, other changes are seen in a depressed person. Most of these changes are characterized by withdrawal.

The depressed individual withdraws in varying degrees from family, friends and customary activity. A person may be able to go through the motions of holding a job or attending a social event—if the depression is not too severe. But he may be unable to maintain the same act at home. Such people may retreat to the quiet of their own room at every opportunity.

Physical signs of depression are also present. A change of appetite is frequently noticed. This is usually a decreased appetite with subsequent loss of weight. Less often there is an increase of appetite with weight gain. Sleep is disturbed, usually with insomnia or early morning wakening with an inability to return to sleep. Sometimes the opposite is true; the patient withdraws to sleep most of the time. Bowel habits often change and constipation may present a problem. Many times depression is the cause of a variety of physical complaints for which no cause can be found by repeated examinations. Abdominal pains, back problems, headaches are a few examples of typical complaints. These physical complaints may be the only symptoms of some depressions, therefore, physicians must be aware that a possible cause for repetitious, unexplained physical complaints may be depression. I will have more to say about this in the chapter on low blood sugar (hypoglycemia).

CHAPTER 2

Depression As Viewed
by the Patient

IN THE CASE of sadness plus hopelessness equaling depression,
the sum is greater than its parts. Sadness by itself is tolerable
and a common experience. If there is an apprehension that
sadness will never change, a new dimension then exists. The
despair of a depressed person can be imagined if you can look
back in your life and remember the lowest point, when everything looked bleak and when nothing was going right at work,
with friends or with the family. Now try to imagine living at
that time and believing that there was a 90 percent chance that
things might change for the better. Try to imagine only a 50
per cent chance for the better; a 25 per cent chance; no chance.
This will give you an idea of how a depressed person feels and
how a depression can move from bad to worse when he loses
hope that things will get better. As the depression becomes
more severe and there is little future but profound sadness, the
idea of suicide becomes stronger and more of a possibility.

The person suffering from depression chooses to withdraw
more and more from his usual activity. Not only does he feel
inadequate and uncomfortable being around others, but also he
has lost interest in things that used to matter to him. At times

work is an impossible chore. Family and friends are ignored and kept at a distance. In the deeper depressions, the patient sees little need for routine hygiene or for taking care of his appearance.

Whatever happens or might happen is regarded with profound pessimism. It is difficult for the depressed person to see the positive in anything. At times this is infuriating to the patient's family, who is faced with this situation day after day.

In addition to these attitudes and behavior patterns during depression, there are some physical changes that often occur. As I have mentioned, there is a change in appetite, bringing either a weight loss or a weight gain. Insomnia may be the first sign that something is wrong. Sleep disturbance takes many forms: inability to fall asleep, frequently waking during the night, or early morning awakening. Sleep disturbances are critical because, in addition to missing the sleep that is necessary to restore mind and body, they give the patient ample time to think black thoughts about the despondency of his depression.

The patient may lose interest in sex. The apathy towards sex when viewed by the patient is seen as a profound and everlasting change and not recognized for what it is: a symptom of depression. As I have noted, some people tell me that their depression is worse at different times of the day; sometimes in the morning and sometimes as the day goes on. This change of the depressed state during the day as well as the type of sleep disturbance experienced may help the doctor in making a careful diagnosis of the type of depression that is present.

The depressed person usually puts himself through many tortures due to misinterpretation and exaggeration. Just as the loss of sexual interest is misconstrued and given an unjust significance, the patient misinterprets life's experiences as evidence of his own worthlessness and self-blame. In addition to cultivating the black side of whatever happens, the patient may resurrect life situations from the distant past in order to confirm the worthlessness, the blame, the bad judgment, the evil intent of the patient. The dredging up of long past events and the misinterpretation of them is characteristic of some depressed states. Most depressions have some degree of worthlessness and self-blame. It is essential that such statements and feelings be recognized as symptoms of an illness and not concentrate on the content of what is said.

A peculiar memory defect is often seen in the depressed person. There seems to be a hopelessness that reaches into the past as well as into the future. For one who is depressed, there is no recognition of past joys. They are remembered as events without the appropriate feelings. It is as if joy never existed. The same lack of memory for good things is present as the patient begins to improve. There may be a good day without any depression, followed by a very depressed day. On a depressed day there is little memory for the pleasant experiences of the previous day. The happy moments, both past and present, seem to be blocked out.

There are three important things that a depressed person can do for himself:

1. Recognize the self-torturing thoughts and physical changes for what they are: symptoms of a disease.

2. Recognize that depression is a disease.

3. Recognize that this disease, like other diseases, can be treated successfully. *You don't have to stay depressed.*

10

CHAPTER 3

Depression as Seen by
Family and Friends

BY OBSERVING the atittudes of the patient, families and friends
often notice signs of depression. Those close to the depressed
person notice ordinary events which should result in some pleasure fail to register. Self accomplishments, compliments, activities and rewards involving family and friends are all without
the usual reaction of joy. In fact, joy, pleasure, happiness are
emotions which become non-existent to the depressed person.
The depressed grandparent avoids his loving grandchild; the
businessman is uninterested and unimpressed by his profits; a
pretty teenager fails to recognize her popularity. All these reactions of depression can be observed by families and friends.

Happiness is replaced by sadness and gloom. A generally
pessimistic outlook will invariably twist a happy event into
something sad. A recital of dire consequences of even happy
times may be observed. For example, the businessman failing
to react to a good profit picture will instead worry about what
might happen in the coming months.

As depression increases, families note the patient is motivated
to do as little as possible. At first there may be less communication within the family; longer periods are spent in tortured,

11

self-imposed solitude. Social activities are minimized and work becomes progressively challenging and demanding. The easiest tasks are deferred. Families may observe an uneven selective withdrawal. In the depressed businessman who must work to support his family, withdrawal may first be noticed at home where no pretenses are necessary. The outgoing, friendly, but depressed breadwinner can often maintain a front necessary for work and essential social engagements while withdrawing from family interaction.

The deception takes on many forms, depending on the patient's priorities. Sometimes this is difficult for families to accept. "If you can talk and be happy at the office, why can't you be happy at home?" The businessman puts up a front at his office; the housewife and mother may put up a front with her children. As depression progresses, families may note that the patient's involvement in other areas deteriorates alarmingly. Withdrawal may involve an ever increasing portion of the patient's current life situation, leading to a preoccupation with past errors, self-blame, expressions of hopelessness, more self involvement and less interest in others. Suicidal thoughts may be seen by the family in varying degrees. The person who is depressed is not feeling, acting or thinking as he should. The spark of life, the pleasure, the desire for self preservation, the caring all diminish. The life machine seems to be stopping and nothing seems to be effective in getting it going. All this is easily observed by families and friends.

What the family can do

Depression is a lonely disease. The sense of isolation and aloneness; the feelings of rejection cause the patient to think, "No one loves me." When a person has reached that stage, even in a home where there is a lot of love, it is difficult to convince him otherwise. An abrupt show of affection may have the opposite effect. His thinking has lost contact with reality and this is another symptom that is useful to the physician. Other times there is a sense of withdrawal, even as the patient accepts the fact that he has a loving and concerned family but is unable to respond to the strong affection and concern. They can also sense the frustration on the part of loved ones who are unable to get through to them. It only serves to give the patient more ammunition for despising himself. "Look what I am doing to my family. They would be better off without me."

Since there are different kinds of depression, just as there are different degrees of depression, there can be no easy 1-2-3 steps in coping with it. Sometimes a lot of help and intervention are required; sometimes very little is needed. Here are the factors that should be weighed:

1. How serious is the depression in terms of interfering with work, family relationships and friendships?

2. How good is the person's judgment and insight? Does he recognize that anything is wrong?

3. How is he trying to help himself? Has he sought outside help? How appropriate is the help he has requested?

4. Is the condition getting better, worse or staying about the same?

5. What is the attitude of the affected person to me?

An assessment of these factors will help the family to decide how much intervention is necessary and how much pressure to apply.

At one end of the spectrum we find a patient who is mildly sad, with only fleeting pangs of hopelessness, who realizes that there is an abnormal situation. He, therefore, seeks appropriate help from friends and/or physician and begins to show an improvement. At the other end is the person who is sad with feelings of absolute hopelessness to a point of lying in bed all day and refusing to eat. In the first example the family can be supportive and loving, while the patient is going through his ordeal and searching intelligently for help. In the second example the family efforts may be lifesaving. But, I must caution, these two extremes represent only a small fraction of the cases that I deal with.

I am always of the opinion that, where family and friends are willing to become involved with the patient's recovery, they should become part of the solution. The patient does not live in a vacuum consisting of a therapist and himself. The people around him should be a part of the recovery plan. Most of the time, when there is a physician involved, it means having an open line of communication between the family and the therapist. Many times families have been surprised and relieved when they have been told of the importance of their involvement and the necessity of being in touch with the physician. So often the families who can be a valuable asset are turned away by the therapist: "You are not my patient. Talking to you will interfere with the therapeutic process." When such an attitude is applied blindly in accord with preconceived principles and not because of a specific situation, the therapist is losing one of his most important contacts.

Recently, a patient of mine, who had been treated successfully over a very tortuous year and with whom I felt I had a good therapeutic relationship, was transferred to another physician at my request. After my disagreement with his father, whose attitude often was not therapeutic, I realized that a very important part of the therapy had been lost and that my effectiveness would have been reduced substantially because I could no longer communicate with his family. I explained this to the patient and the transfer was arranged. There have been other instances when I felt a family member was more destructive than helpful. In those situations, which have been very few, I have told my patient that I would continue as their physician only if that particular member of the family had no access to the therapy. Most of the time this happens at the request of the patient, who may say: "My father is nuts. I'm not with him and I don't want anything to do with him." If there is reason to believe that this is true and the patient is free from the physical presence and is independent, there would be no advantage in bringing the family members into the situation against the will of the patient. The point I wish to make is that each situation must be judged individually. In my experience at least, it is rare to exclude the family from treatment.

The family can sometimes be effective when they learn that the patient is unwilling to seek help. They must try to convince him that he is ill and needs the guidance of a trained therapist. It is like an alcoholic, who generally does not make any progress in controlling the disease until he realizes that he is an alcoholic. Of course, it is not always easy to bring the patient and the psychiatrist together. Many patients object to the prevalent idea that all diseases treated by the psychologist are psychological in origin. Such a reluctant patient can be seen to be more cooperative in seeking help from a physician who is able to approach the emotional symptom with a medical and/or nutritional approach, which is a valid treatment in some depressions.

Most physicians feel that it is the right of every mentally ill person to receive medical attention. In some instances the symptoms of the illness are poor judgment, lack of insight, fear and mistrust, etc., so that the family and physician, in order to provide the necessary medical help, must do it against the patient's will. There is an outspoken, minority group of psychiatrists who regard any invasion of the rights of the individual as inexcusable. They feel that a person who is ill should not be subject to treatment against his wishes.

I am strongly against such a perverted concept of personal liberty. A patient who is hopelessly lost in depression has a distorted viewpoint. It may be that simple vitamin therapy and a corrective diet, along with a minimum of therapeutic aids, can quickly and inexpensively return this patient to a productive life. Without this treatment, his life may be completely wasted. Unfortunately, legislatures throughout the United States, all too eager to jump on the personal liberty bandwagon, have enacted such restrictive legislation that, in protecting the rights of a few, they have endangered the rights of the majority. The significance of this unwise legislation is that, if you are unfortunate enough to have a mentally ill relative who refuses all types of help, there is little that can be done legally to help them, unless there is a very clear danger that this person may bring harm to himself or to others.

Besides getting appropriate professional care, one of the most important ways a family can help is in attitude. Throughout the illness there should be a prevailing feeling that "We recognize that you have an illness and fortunately something can be done about it." With some people there is a carry over of a feeling of shame connected with any illness that is within the province of psychiatry. Whenever possible, such an attitude should be dismissed. My own feeling is that many depressions are medical in origin and as such should be subject to no more shame than having pneumonia or an allergy.

Families can help enormously by acquainting themselves with the importance of diet and the possible need for food supplements while gently persuading the patient to seek competent medical help. Obviously a patient who shuts himself off from the family and refuses to eat is risking further complications. Without the proper nutrition, the ability of the mind to handle problems is compromised. Other medical diseases may develop. Weight loss and weakness may confuse the picture. In addition, it is known that proper protein ingestion is necessary for the functioning of some of the common anti-depressant medications.

The patient is not the only one to suffer. In *Megavitamin Therapy*, Ruth Adams and Frank Murray tell the story of a 21-year-old woman from a wealthy family who began to display

16

peculiar symptoms a month after graduating from a fashionable college. She had hallucinations and would repeat meaningless gestures over and over. Psychiatrists diagnosed schizophrenia and, in a period of five years, she was in and out of seven medical centers, all to no avail.

Joan was finally taken to a psychiatrist who believes in megavitamin therapy. He told the family that she was suffering from pellagra, the vitamin B3 deficiency disease. This came about, it turned out, when Joan went on a crash diet one month before graduating. Her physician prescribed amphetamines, which are supposed to curb the appetite. Joan ate almost nothing and was losing about 12 pounds a week. She found that the pep pills could keep her going almost indefinitely without eating, so this gave her more time to stay awake at night and cram for exams. The strain on her nutritional reserves was such that pellagra developed. But the long road to this realization had cost the family $230,000 and virtually bankrupt them, not to mention their despair watching the suffering of their child.

"Joan's pellagra and her schizoid symptoms have now disappeared as the result of a carefully supervised diet, fortified with heavy doses of ascorbic acid (vitamin C), niacin and other vitamins of the B complex," wrote Norman Cousins in the December 10, 1972 issue of the *Philadelphia Inquirer.*

Well-meaning families will often counsel the person who is ill to "Get out, do something, you'll feel better." Such a command implies to the patient that the illness and remedy are completely under his own control. Further there is the implication that if you are depressed it is because you want it that way. This advice inevitably backfires because the patient already feels guilty about the illness and he becomes even more guilty when he is unable to help himself as directed. The patient may also sense the frustration and disgust of the family, which only adds to his burden.

Anyone who has ever been depressed will tell you that no

one wants to be depressed. If anything could be done to get out of the depression, they would certainly do it. "Pulling yourself up by the boot straps" is not the usual way out of a depressed state. So all the advice to "snap out of it," "what have you got to be depressed about?" "smile," "take care of yourself," "get busy and you'll feel better," etc., is not only ineffective but usually makes things worse.

The kind of help the family can offer depends on the stage of the illness. There are three times during the illness when family can help: at the earliest signs, during the illness, and in the recovery phase. Help in each of these stages is different. In the beginning, seek professional advice. Of course, when there is no previous pattern, it will be difficult to recognize the earliest signs. A deepening withdrawal, sadness and hopelessness should start to clarify the picture of a depression. In some depressions there is the repetition of symptoms, behavior and thought, which usher in a depressive episode. In those cases the family can be very helpful by recognizing the symptoms and getting help early.

During the illness

The attitudes that I have discussed are important and should be maintained throughout the illness. The hopelessness of depression makes a person feel like they will always be that way. Often there is no recognition that life was ever any different. Especially when there has been a past history of illness, it can be supportive for family and friends to emphasize that there has always been an improvement before and such a change could surely be expected in the present illness. Past accomplishments and positive relationships might be pointed out to those who have forgotten any positive aspects of their life.

During the illness the family can supply not only the positive attitude discussed, but also on a more practical basis be certain that the treatment as outlined by the physician is followed. For example, if the doctor has found the patient's diet lacking and has suggested the elimination of many refined carbohydrates and "junk" foods, it is the family's obligation to help the patient carry out these orders. If vitamin supplements have been recommended, then it is up to the family to see that an ample supply is always at hand. Sometimes there is the attitude on the part of the family that, if the person is to get well, he must arrange for his own medication, own treatment and whatever else the physician has ordered. When the patient is *able* to do these things, he should be encouraged to help himself. But family members should realize that sometimes the illness prevents such self-sufficient activity. In those cases it is imperative that the family helps.

The recovery phase

When the patient starts to improve, a different approach should be taken by the family. Characteristically the improvement is not like flicking a switch from darkness to light and remaining that way. The patient may experience a dramatic change of feeling. Many times patients have described a sensation "as if a veil had been lifted." Unfortunately, more often than not, this dramatic return to health does not continue ever upward without interruption.

The meaning of the breaks in the depressed feeling, even if short-lived, is that some positive changes are taking place and the healing process is working. The healing period from depression to health may be compared to what happens in the transition of a completely gray sky to a beautifully clear blue sky. At first there is nothing but gray, then a break in the clouds reveals a clear fleck of blue sky. Failing to take an overall view and limiting your vision to a very small area of the sky at that time, you would describe the sky as blue, which, of course, is an obvious error. This is the type of error made by some patients, who experience the first break in depression and feel that they are completely well. A more objective analysis reveals a very small patch of blue in a predominantly overcast sky. As clearing progresses, more and more patches of blue appear and the gray begins to disappear. The balance is changing. Finally, there is a very small trace of gray in a predominantly blue sky. The balance has reversed itself.

It is important that the patient knows where he is in an overall viewpoint. This is to prevent the usual series of feelings that occur when they fail to take the proper perspective. At the first substantial sign of health, the patient is prompted to exclaim, "Thank God, it's over. I'm well again." The following day, when he feels as depressed as ever, he is apt to think, "I'm never going to get well." It is this frustration at the loss of having any good feelings that now begins to complicate an already distressing situation. The development of the hope prompted by the good day and the distress, disgust and resignation that follow the loss of the good day are sometimes more stressful than an already fragile person can tolerate.

To remember these ups and downs and to take an overall view of the situation is difficult for a patient unassisted. At this point the family's intervention in putting the day-to-day experiences in perspective can be very helpful and may prevent a prolongation of the depression due to having to deal with added disappointments. When the patient experiences a return of depression and is convinced that he will never get well, it is helpful for the family to point out that this up and down period is to be expected and is quite normal. Direct statements can be helpful, such as, "You were feeling so much better yesterday. I'm sure that will come again." The family is able to see the day-to-day changes in the illness as part of an overall picture. The patient who experiences the pain often loses this important viewpoint and sees each day as forever. Today is like yesterday and tomorrow will be like today. It is up to the family to supply reality and give hope where hope does exist.

DEPRESSION AS SEEN BY FAMILY AND FRIENDS

Therefore, to recap, the family can help throughout the depression by their attitude. By recognizing that depression is an illness and that it is unwanted by the hopeless patient, the family can intervene where necessary to secure proper help. After that, the family must cooperate with the physician to see that the treatment plan is followed. At the same time they can offer encouragement so that an end to the depression may be seen based on real expectations. In this respect, the family becomes a very important part of the total therapy, whether it is seeing that the proper medication is taken, or whether it is supplying a recommended diet regime or food supplements.

Family and friends are in the best position, usually, to recognize and take appropriate action against the ultimate danger of severe depression—suicide.

CHAPTER 4

Suicide—the Ultimate
Danger of Depression

"THE HIGH INCIDENCE of suicide makes it a strong possibility in sudden death," states *The Book of Health* (third edition), by Dr. Randolph Lee Clark and Dr. Russell W. Cumley. "Often the very points which seem to rule out suicide to the lay mind are those which medicolegal experts recognize as strongly suggestive of self-destruction. . . . It is estimated from past data that 21 males and 7 females out of every 1,000 born will eventually take their own lives. Male suicides outnumber females about three to one. However, women attempt suicide more often than men, but are less successful. . . .

"There are more suicides in urban areas than in rural areas and suicides occur most often in spring and summer. There are many motives for suicide, and they are often obscure. The reasons most often indicated are ill health, economic distress, loss of a loved one and domestic discord. The final circumstances leading to suicide may not be closely related to the underlying cause, but may point to a long chain of contributory events," *The book of Health* continues.

The latter observation might possibly explain the death of a young socialite and heir to a large fortune on May 7, 1975 in

SUICIDE—THE ULTIMATE DANGER OF DEPRESSION

New York City. While visiting the United Nations, a tourist heard gunshots and reported this to police. They arrived at a secluded spot on the UN grounds, there to find that the young man, 34, had apparently shot himself between the eyes. A gun and a suicide note were nearby.

The note, as reported by the *New York Post*, read in part: "The defense of the planet against contamination by radioactive materials is the most important task of mankind now or in the foreseeable future, and it may be immensely more difficult and expensive than is even imagined now. Remember: The Geneva Accords, the nonproliferation treaty, the UN Charter. America's promises must be kept . . . especially the good ones."

Since little more is known about the man's background, except that he was a writer, one can only speculate that his death was a protest against what he considered monumental problems. Such violent protests, often with political overtones, were indicative of the 1970s. In fact, Sam Heilig, executive director of the Los Angeles Suicide Prevention Center said, in the April 3, 1972 issue of *The New York Times*: "I've never known a generation as interested in death as an experience, something you can pass through."

Mr. Heilig, who was addressing the annual convention of the American Association of Suicidology in Detroit, reports that, while suicides among the elderly—especially old, white men, a normally high-risk area—are falling off, those for the young, particularly among women, are on the increase.

The convention was told that approximately 25,000 people, or 11 for each 100,000 population, kill themselves each year in the United States. Some experts in the field, however, believe that the rate may be twice that number.

The possibility of suicide in the very depressed person is, of course, always present. Since family and friends may be the first to get the message from the patient, they should know how

23

to interpret the telltale signs. The best answer: interpret the message seriously.

There is a popular misconception which states, "If you talk about suicide, you don't do it." This is wrong. In most suicides the intention is clear long before it happens. Of course, not every person marches into the living room and announces his suicide plan. There are often several attempts before a successful suicide is accomplished. So when there is a history of suicide attempts: Beware!

If there is not a direct statement about the patient's intentions, there may be a clear indication from his conversation and behavior. Sometimes notes are left so that they purposely can be found. Pills may be hidden and stored until enough are available for the attempts. This is especially true of women, who generally choose the less disfiguring forms of suicide.

So the patient's intentions may be blunt or minimally disguised. It is as if some suicidal patients want to play a game of Russian roulette. They leave clues, they make an attempt where there is a chance that they will be found and saved. Implied is the chance that they won't. The person who is absolutely intent on suicide makes certain that he has a foolproof method when he is alone and not apt to be found until it is too late. Of course, many suicide attempts are done half heartedly at a time and place where there is a chance that they will be saved. Unfortunately, this is a dangerous game because quite often they are not found in time. It is primarily in this group where alertness and professional help may be life-saving. The person is asking for help. So give it.

I should say that a special precaution should be exercised if there is a strong family history of suicide. Where there is such a history in a person who is depressed, everyone should be aware that there is an added danger, even if suicidal thoughts have not been expressed.

The extent of suicide in this country can only be estimated.

24

SUICIDE—THE ULTIMATE DANGER OF DEPRESSION

The 25,000 figure that I reported are usually the obvious cases. But there are many more deaths which are probably arranged to look like accidents, such as pedestrians being hit by cars and drownings. These victims are classified as "accidental deaths."

There are approximately 10 times as many suicide attempts as there are suicides each year. In 1964, Dr. Ronald Mintz estimated from a public health survey in Los Angeles that there were five million Americans with suicidal history. This provides for a large reservoir of potentially successful suicides.

When there is a family history of suicide, those close to the patient must be ever vigilant. For example, I know the case of a young woman whose father jumped off a Staten Island ferry when she was very young, leaving her behind. This traumatic event has been on her mind all these years (she is now in her thirties), therefore, it is not unexpected that she should try suicide, since she often related the childhood experience. She took an overdose of sleeping pills but managed to telephone a friend in time to be saved. Since she was not my patient I do not know her medical history, but I do know that the suicide attempt came when she was depressed about losing a job. A new job was not working out. Inclined to be overweight, she was always on a crash weight-reducing program. I suspect this program, which probably deprived her body of sufficient nutrition, helped to trigger her depression and the inevitable attempt to kill herself.

Statistics can provide some information about the group of people most likely to attempt suicide, but statistics are not always reliable. Statistics do classify the potential suicides as: 1) Suicide rate is twice as high in middle-aged men as it is in the same age group for women. 2) As men get older the rate stays high, but the successful suicide rate in women decreases after the middle years. 3) The figures for "attempted" suicide show that more women of all ages attempt suicide. With apologies to feminists, this seems to be an undisputed area in which men are more successful. 4) There is a rise in the suicide rate among adolescents and college students, which has made suicide the third most common cause of death among young adults. 5) There is a suggestion that the person who attempts suicide and is also a heavy user of alcohol will have a greater chance of being successful in the attempt.

Not much comfort can be found in statistics when it comes to judging each individual. Even though the rate is high in men, women and young adults also commit suicide. While the chance for successful suicide is higher in alcoholics, those who are alcohol-free also commit suicide. Obviously, other factors must be considered with each individual case.

Suicide usually occurs when a person is suffering from an overwhelming depression and in schizophrenics. The feeling of complete hopelessness about ever enjoying anything but the intense sadness is the state of depression that leads easily to suicidal thoughts and attempts. Those afflicted with schizophrenia may hear voices commanding them to kill themselves or to jump from high places, which, of course, also results in their death. Schizophrenics may also be significantly depressed and commit suicide when despondent.

I recall a young schizophrenic man who had been depressed for many months. He began to respond to a change in his treatment and, for the first time in months, began to join his family for dinner and in other activities. He began to laugh, joke and show interest in his previous pursuits. This change took place rapidly within one week. After one evening of "being like his old self," according to his mother, he was found dead with a plastic bag wrapped around his head. Suicides which occur when the patient is showing definite improvement are, in my experience, the most difficult to predict and the most frustrating and heartbreaking for the family and physician. After a long period of illness, just as there appears to be a breakthrough, tragedy occurs.

There are a few possible explanations for this seeming contradiction. One explanation is that the patient who has been so depressed and has considered suicide literally did not have the energy to do so until there was some improvement in his health. Another explanation is that the patient finally decides that suicide is the only solution. For example, a patient who has had difficulty in thinking and feeling decides to solve his problem by suicide, and, having made a decision about a difficult situation, the patient appears relieved and seems improved.

To protect against this type of suicide is the most difficult, since, in these cases, having resolved to use suicide as a solution, the patient usually doesn't discuss his intentions and the tragedy occurs at a time when it is least expected and least understood. About the only precaution is that, if a patient's condition improves too rapidly and everything seems to be going too good, caution should be observed.

There are other factors that make suicide likely. An important part of the history, as we know, is whether or not there have been any suicides in the family. Such a history makes suicide more likely. Previous suicide attempts should always be taken seriously, since this is an indication of what is on the patient's mind. Drug users are also potential suicide victims due to an overdose, drug intoxication or hallucinations brought on by the use of drugs. Sometimes these patients will respond to false visions, voices or thoughts just as the schizophrenic does. In the 1960s, during the height of the LSD craze, there were numerous deaths due to this drug, such as walking through a sixth-floor window, thinking it was a ground floor door, or jumping from a height in an attempt to fly.

The patient who is a dangerous suicidal threat must be watched every minute. Most of the time this cannot be done adequately at home; sometimes not even in a hospital. Some people are so determined that, no matter what is done to prevent it, they manage to kill themselves. Dr. Stephen Smith, a former director of Gracie Square Hospital in New York, related the story of a young navy man who was on a 24-hour constant observation because of a suicide attempt. He finally managed to succeed by going to the bathroom in a small private toilet stall with a swinging door. His attendant felt that it was unnecessary to observe the young man and so allowed him to close the swinging door. While the attendant was standing nearby, the man stood on the toilet seat and dove head first onto the tile floor, breaking his neck and dying immediately.

This, of course, is an extreme example, but it does serve to illustrate the determination that some distressed people have. Therefore, every effort must be made to save patients from suicide. This may sound strange but it is said with emphasis because there are some psychiatrists who believe that anyone has the right to suicide. I feel that such beliefs are dangerous and misleading, even though they may attract some adherents. I doubt that anyone with enough hopelessness to commit suicide would want to die if he were well. In attempting suicide, he is acting under duress and with poor judgment.

For those cases of depression and schizophrenia who have a reasonable chance of improvement, it is the duty of the physician to treat the illness and not retire behind some intellectual dogma about individual rights. Some reasonable and humane argument might be made for a person's right to choose his own death when faced with an uncontrollable or incurable disease, but neither depression nor schizophrenia fits into that classification.

To prevent suicides, those who care the most for the potential victim must be able to recognize when a real threat exists. They should then either take the patient to competent professional help or seek the help of a professional as to the best course to take. In the larger cities, Suicide Prevention centers have counsellors who can be telephoned for help.

In my own practice, I have seen countless potential suicides saved through the various methods that I have described in this book. In many cases, once the depression is gone—along with the insomnia, hopelessness, self-doubt, etc.—and the patient is returned to good health there is no reason to think of suicide as a solution. But in a depressed state, feeling hopeless that life will ever improve, a patient may see suicide as the only alternative.

With the competent medical, psychiatric and nutritional help that is available in almost every community in the United States, suicide can be prevented in most cases. This can best be accomplished with the help of an understanding family and friends.

CHAPTER 5

Depression as Seen
by the Physician

THE WORK OF the physician is to heal the sick, but healing is not synonymous with relieving symptoms: symptoms may be relieved without healing. A headache may be relieved with aspirin but there may be several causes of the headache, which go undiagnosed and therefore untreated. Repeated vomiting may be stopped by the use of tranquilizers, but the cause of the vomiting—such as an infection or an ulcer—will not be influenced by tranquilization.

In dealing with depression, the physician must first diagnose the disease then direct the patient through the treatment that is most likely to succeed. In thinking about depression, it becomes obvious to even the most casual observer that, although the depressions share similar symptoms in different degrees, the causes of the depression vary tremendously. An effort must be made by the physician to unravel the causes so that the right treatment can be instituted.

The initial work of the physician is obviously to find out what is wrong with the patient. The process of diagnosing depression follows the same pattern as the diagnosis of any other illness; namely, the collection of signs and symptoms; the use of laboratory techniques to aid in diagnosis and treatment. All illnesses have specific signs and symptoms. The symptoms are what the patient experiences. He can tell someone about his complaints but the experience is entirely his. No one can experience your headache, stiff joint or sore throat. The signs of an illness are thus observed by the physician. The patient may complain of a sore throat (a symptom), but the physician may observe a high temperature, flushing of the skin, facial expression of pain on swallowing, enlargement and sensitivity to pain in the glands of the neck, rapid pulse, weakness and a bright red throat.

Therefore, the diagnostic process begins with the collection of data. The necessary information may be obtained from the patient or others who have observed him. After asking a patient for his complaints, the symptoms, the physician is also interested in the signs as noted by the patient and other observers. The physician then augments his own data by doing a physical examination. Through this process he begins to suspect—or in some cases know—what the nature of the problem is. All types of laboratory studies may be utilized to give a clearer picture of what is wrong. It is during this time that a physician who suspects the depression may be related to nutrition may inquire what the person is eating and whether or not he takes food supplements. The doctor can thus determine whether or not a change in diet may be an avenue of approach, along with other psychiatric aids to treat the depression.

Most of the time the indication of depression is obvious because the patient indicates that he is depressed. He may amplify his concern thus:

1. "Life seems entirely hopeless."
2. "I usually feel miserable and blue."
3. "My thinking gets all mixed up when I have to act quickly."
4. "Sometimes the world becomes very dim and confused to me."

5. "I am keyed up and constantly jittery."
6. "I often suffer from severe nervous exhaustion."
7. "My friends often irritate me."
8. "I have trouble getting my work done on time."
9. "Nothing interests me anymore."
10. "Life doesn't seem worth living."
11. "I have to push myself to get anything done."
12. "I'd like to go to sleep and never wake up."
13. "I am often shaky."
14. "I have difficulty falling asleep at night."
15. "My family doesn't understand me."
16. "I am always tired."
17. "The days seem to go by very slowly."
18. "I usually feel alone and sad at a party."
19. "I cannot make up my mind about things that didn't trouble me before."
20. "My life seems terribly disorganized."

These are common complaints of the depressed person. In such instances, it is redundant to announce to the patient and his family that he is depressed. They already know it. What the patient wants to know is what can be done about it. In order to answer that question the physician must get to the root of the trouble before treatment can begin.

This is where the difficulty arises. There is no universal agreement among professionals engaged in the mental health field as to what causes depression. There is similar confusion about the cause of most illnesses of a psychiatric nature. Those doctors trained in a center which stresses psychological causes of mental illness will be more prone to see the psychological aspects of the symptoms presented by the patient. Physicians trained to recognize medical causes for mental illness might underestimate the psychological causes. And those specialists who favor a nutritional approach to depression and other forms

32

of mental illnesses may try their treatment before considering any other modalities.

When there is success with a specific treatment, there is little controversy between the specialists. There may be disagreements about nuances of the treatment, but there is very little difference of opinion as to the correct approach. On the other hand, when no one treatment approach has proved to be universally successful, tempers may flare. When such a situation arises, it is safe to assume that no one school has the complete answer. If cooler heads can prevail, a less agitated dialogue can begin which will benefit everyone.

Such a confrontation is most likely in dealing with mental illnesses. Factions arise, each strongly divided between the physical causes and the psychological causes. Ideally, the medically oriented physician should be aware of the psychological needs of his patient. Conversely, the psychologically oriented physician should be aware of the possible medical causes of the patient's disease. And both camps should be aware that there exists a nutritionally oriented faction, but, unfortunately, this latter group is often derided and ignored. In essence, physicians from these three groups should learn from each other. The causes of mental illness are complex, involving psychological, medical and nutritional aspects. The physician must determine the relative importance of the causes before instituting effective treatment.

If the physician is looking for the possibility of both medical and psychological causes when he is collecting the patient's historical data, the investigation he undertakes will confirm or tend to disprove his suspicions. He must have an open mind to all causes or he will only see what he wishes to see. After determining that the patient is indeed depressed, the physician must gather more facts. "Is there anything to be depressed about?" is a logical beginning. If there has been a death in the family or indeed any kind of loss—a financial loss, the loss of a friend, the loss of a job, etc.—and the depression followed that loss, then there is a good chance that psychological reasons are at the basis of the symptoms. Of course, all of us suffer losses from time to time but manage to cope with them.

The answer as to why some people succumb to these losses and others do not is probably found in an analysis of the psychological and medical factors in the person's life. Other questions to be considered are the age and sex of the patient at the onset of the problem and whether or not there is a history of depression. Have there ever been any episodes of an elated feeling or behavior, related or unrelated to real events? Is there any family history of mood disturbances? What is the state of the patient's health? Are there any acute or chronic illnesses? Is there any evidence of an endocrine (gland) disorder, such as thyroid or sex hormones? What is the state of the patient's nutrition? Are there any eating peculiarities or cravings?

The physician must also be aware of other physical or environmental factors which might influence the symptoms. What are the living conditions of the patient? Is he able to care for himself or are others caring for him? Does he have any financial worries? Is he able and willing to accept suggestions? Are there any life threatening factors, such as fasting or suicidal threats or attempts? The answers to these questions enable the physician to determine the setting for treatment: home, hospital, or half-way house, and the kind of treatment.

The proper treatment, of course, depends on the skill of the physician. So much is unknown about psychiatric treatment that no responsible professional can be opinionated about a particular approach. As I have indicated, there are many kinds of depression and it is the responsibility of the physician, the expert, to define the particular kind of depression and what can best be done about it. It is not the duty of the patient to make his own diagnosis. The wise patient and his family will seek out a broadminded physician who will plan a treatment based on the patient's psychological and medical needs. If one realizes that there are many causes of depression and many avenues of attack, then a physician can be chosen on the basis of the thoroughness of his approach.

In a later chapter I will give some suggestions as to how to choose a doctor.

PART 2

Hypoglycemia

CHAPTER 6

How Nutritional Therapy Works

"IF THE BROMIDE, 'You are what you eat,' is true, we could all end up being very different people from our ancestors," writes Michael Jacobson in the April, 1975 issue of *Smithsonian*. "Modern science and agriculture have freed the United States and many other nations from traditional diets based largely on natural farm products. New varieties of crops, transcontinental shipping, a wide spectrum of food additives, and new food-processing techniques have led, for better or worse, to diets different from any previously consumed by human populations. But these dietary changes reflect the decisions of business executives and investors, rather than nutritionists and public health officials.

"The United States," Mr. Jacobson continues, "not surprisingly, has been the leader in the genetic engineering of food crops and in the laboratory creation of new foods. Benjamin Franklin and Abraham Lincoln, if they could visit us, would probably have some difficulty distinguishing between a toy store and a supermarket. They would not even recognize as foods such products as artificial whipped cream in its pressurized can, or some of the breakfast 'cereals' that are almost half sugar and

39

bear little resemblance to cereal grains. Franklin and Lincoln would probably feel much more at home in the homey 'natural foods' stores that are popping up everywhere than they would in the 10,000-item supermarkets. Many of the new foods do save us time and trouble, but they are often costly, in terms of both dollars and, ultimately, health.''

Although I cannot state categorically that these new convenience foods are a major cause of depression and other forms of mental illness, they are certainly a contributing factor in some cases. Many factors enter the picture with regard to a person's mental health—general health, environment, day-to-day stresses, heredity, etc.—but, obviously, nutrition is also an important key.

Brian Weiss, writing in the December, 1974 issue of *Psychology Today*, states: '' 'You are what you eat' may turn out to be as true behaviorally as it is bodily. What you are eating may also be what is eating you, and the relation between a six o'clock dinner and a seven o'clock diatribe may be more causal than casual.''

Mr. Weiss goes on to say that food supplies the amino acids, or forms of protein, from which the brain makes many of its neurotransmitters. These are the chemicals that carry information from neuron to neuron (a nerve cell), affecting movement and mood as information is stored and sorted in millions of places simultaneously.

"The production of neurochemicals in the brain was once thought to be insulated from the meal-to-meal vagaries of amino acid intake," Mr. Weiss continues. "Recent research, however, concludes that what you eat is what you get . . . and perhaps how you act.''

Mrs. Weiss reports that Richard Wurtman, John Fernstrom and several colleagues at the Massachusetts Institute of Technology have found that the availability of two amino acids (tyrosine and tryptophan) in the brain is a major factor in determining the rate at which four neurotransmitters are produced. Within one hour after a meal, the levels of these chemicals begin to change as the amounts of tyrosine and tryptophan in the blood rise and fall, Mr. Weiss adds.

"Tyrosine and tryptophan must compete with three other amino acids for the limited places available on the transit system from blood to brain. As the ratio between these amino acids fluctuates, the likelihood of getting a ride into the brain changes, much as the odds at a racetrack change as each bet is placed. When the researchers fed a group of rats a diet high in tryptophan but without competing amino acids, the brain content of the neurotransmitter serotonin, and the tryptophan from which it is produced, rose substantially. The rats that ate food containing competing amino acids, however, showed no increase in the amount of brain tryptophan and serotonin; there were not enough seats on the brain train," Mr. Weiss says.

Serotonin is thought to be associated with the neurons that control sleep, mood and body temperature, and either too much or too little could cause behavioral changes, Mr. Weiss states.

"Long term undernutrition can also have a marked effect on brain neurotransmitters. The MIT researchers showed that there was a deficit in the amount of two neurotransmitters in the brains of rats fed low-protein diets from birth to weaning. While the evidence for humans is necessarily indirect . . . the researchers believe a similar depletion occurs in humans short of protein, and this may well account for the characteristic behavioral symptoms involving lethargy, withdrawal and indifference.

"There are many maybes at the moment, but our understanding of the interaction of human nutrition and human behavior seems tightly bound to progress in finding out about a half dozen chemicals that almost nobody knows," Mr. Weiss concludes.

For those of us who use orthomolecular psychiatry in the treatment of depression and various types of mental illnesses, nutrition is an important element in whether or not the therapy will be successful. Just as sedatives may be necessary to calm the more agitated patients, a definitive nutritional program may be necessary to correct hypoglycemia or some other nutritionally oriented illness.

Orthomolecular psychiatry is a concept defined by Dr. Linus Pauling in an article, "Orthomolecular Psychiatry," in the April 19, 1968 issue of *Science*. He defines orthomolecular psychiatric therapy as "the treatment of mental disease by the provision of the optimum molecular environment for the mind, especially the optimum concentration of substances normally present in the human body."

In the early 1950s, Drs. Abram Hoffer and Humphry Osmond, while working together in a Canadian hospital, were dissatisfied with the treatment of schizophrenia. At the time, all that was available to help these devastatingly ill patients were heavy sedation, shock treatments, psychotherapy, and, for a large proportion of patients, chronic hospitalization. During hospitalization there were a variety of mechanical control measures, such as the traditional straitjacket. This is a shirt made of heavy canvas. It has long sleeves and is put on backwards. The sleeves are tied in the back so that the patient is restrained in a tight, self-hugging position. Other mechanical devices were used for those too wild to move about, such as straps that kept the patient tied to his bed. Hot baths, cold baths and water hoses were also utilized. Needless to say these measures may have forced the patient to conform to the hospital's strict regimentation, but they hardly got to the root of his problem.

Drs. Hoffer and Osmond, disillusioned by the lack of a meaningful treatment for the schizophrenic, developed a theory that would employ large doses (megadoses) of vitamin B3 (niacin) and vitamin C (ascorbic acid). The thesis proposed was that, in the schizophrenic patient, there was a biochemical abnormality that resulted in the buildup of a chemical which caused the symptoms of schizophrenia. Through consideration of the biochemistry involved, they deduced that, by using massive doses of vitamin B3 and vitamin C, the abnormal chemical accumulation would be kept at a level below that necessary for symptom production.

In their clinical trials with cases that had been considered chronic and hopeless, there was enough change noted to encourage further trials and use of this method. While the professional world remained skeptical, there were a few physicians who began to use this approach as an addition to other treatments. An exchange of ideas among the megavitamin therapists contributed to the knowledge. The development of this treatment, in the 1950s, was at a time when "mega" was easily applied to anything that was a bit larger than usual.

But these physicians were adding more than vitamins to the program. Many patients were noted to have low blood sugar and were put on a low-carbohydrate diet. Besides other vitamins, the importance of minerals and trace minerals was realized and these substances are now considered in the treatment. Special amino acids are also sometimes used.

By 1968, when Dr. Pauling wrote his article, the original treatment had about as much resemblance to 1968 megavitamin treatment as the original Chevrolet built by Durant has to the present General Motors Chevrolet. Dr. Pauling crystallized the treatment concept of the then megavitamin therapists, who are now the orthomolecular therapists who attempt, in their treatment, to provide the optimum molecular environment for the mind, especially in using substances NORMALLY PRESENT in the body. In 1973, Dr. Pauling and Dr. David Hawkins edited a medical textbook, *Orthomolecular Psychiatry, Treatment of Schizophrenia* (W.H. Freeman and Company, San Francisco), which contains the professional experience of some of the nation's leading megavitamin therapists.

There is a great deal of misunderstanding, among both professionals and non-professionals, about orthomolecular psychiatry. One of the most pronounced misunderstandings is the belief that orthomolecular psychiatry and the usual practice of psychiatry are mutually exclusive. This is false. What is done in this treatment is an attempt to concentrate on the substances which are usually present in the body (vitamins, minerals, amino acids, etc.), and to use other medications where necessary and only as long as necessary. Psychotherapy is used when advisable, and an attempt is made to use the approach that best suits the patient's needs at the moment.

It may be in this area of psychotherapy that so much misunderstanding and bad feelings have been generated. For a number of years, in the United States at least, psychiatry was dominated by psychoanalysts. Consequently, during this time when a patient consulted a psychiatrist he was treated with an approach that incorporated psychoanalytic ideas. But studies have been done which show the futility of trying to treat acute schizophrenia with analytic therapy. Pure analytic therapy is not often used any more to treat schizophrenia, but there are a few treatment centers where old ideas die hard.

It has always been interesting to me that those who criticize the orthomolecular approach because of lack of evidence showing its effectiveness choose to ignore the studies which spotlighted the ineffectiveness (and in some cases even harm) of an analytically oriented psychotherapy with schizophrenics. It would be an absurdity to state that psychotherapy is worthless. Psychotherapy is a valuable tool, but only when the right kind of psychotherapy is used at the right time.

In my practice I find repeatedly that orthomolecular treatment is sometimes necessary before effective psychotherapy can be employed. In some cases orthomolecular psychiatry is all that is necessary. It is always important to design the treatment for the patient, leaving no areas unexplored that might be beneficial. It is in this area, that of tailoring the treatment to the patient's needs, that the orthomolecular psychiatrist is most frustrated, because so many of our colleagues dismiss the possible use of megavitamin therapy with arrogance, ridicule and prejudice. Throughout this book I have mentioned patients of mine and others who have been successfully treated with orthomolecular psychiatry. Numerous magazine articles and books— e.g., *How to Live with Schizophrenia*, by Dr. Abram Hoffer and Dr. Humphry Osmond—corroborate the effectiveness of this approach. A good list of books, audio tapes, and magazine and journal reprints covering this subject is available from

The Huxley Institute for Biosocial Research
900 North Federal Highway
Boca Raton, FL 33432
1-800 847-3802
407 393-6167

I think it is the immovability of some in the psychiatric community that explains the loss of esteem that psychiatry is now suffering. Prejudice and lack of objectivity have resulted in the dismissal of a valuable psychiatric tool.

In an editorial in *Psychiatric News*, the official newspaper of the American Psychiatric Association (March 19, 1975, Vol. 10, No. 6), the Committee on Public Information decried the continued criticism of psychiatry and especially the responses of psychiatrists to criticism. We, as psychiatrists, are reminded by that editorial that the first constitutional objective of the Association is "to improve the treatment, rehabilitation and care of the mentally ill, the mentally retarded and the emotionally disturbed."

The time has come for the orthomolecular psychiatrists and general psychiatrists to realize that we have a common meeting ground in the needs of our patients. There are many effective psychiatric treatments. It is the duty of the psychiatrist to know these treatments and to prescribe the right treatment for the patient who consults him as an expert in mental health. Shock treatment is not a good treatment for every psychiatric patient. Psychotherapy is not a good treatment for every psychiatric patient. Vitamins are not the sole answer to many psychiatric problems. But as psychiatrists we must know what treatment may be useful and when to use it. We must stop holding to any narrow viewpoint as the answer to all psychiatric problems. The field of psychiatry has grown tremendously and rapidly. It is time that we as psychiatrists do the same.

Although orthomolecular psychiatry began as a treatment for schizophrenia, the conditions that are now treated by this approach are much broader. Patients presenting complaints of depression and anxiety have been benefited by the orthomolecular psychiatrist, as I have demonstrated. Some alcoholics and drug addicts have shown improvement, as reported by Dr. David Hawkins and others. My friend and colleague, Dr. Allan Cott, has shown the suitability of megavitamin therapy in treating problem children, especially those who are hyperactive and have learning disorders.

In my experience as an orthomolecular psychiatrist, I find that many patients who complain of depression have hypoglycemia (low blood sugar). Because hypoglycemia is, in my opinion, so prevalent and causes so much misery and is so misunderstood, I feel it is mandatory to consider the possibility of this disorder whenever a patient complains of depression. Hypoglycemia may be a contributing factor to the depression, and, in some cases, it may be the total cause.

CHAPTER 7

Are You Tired of Being Tired?
Maybe You Have
Hypoglycemia?

"WHEN A CUTE, chubby, 11-year-old boy tells me he talks to his grandfather, I ordinarily do not think much about it. But when Mitch said it, his parents flashed a resigned and resentful look at each other. I did not need any of my psychiatric training to tell me that much more than a casual chat was involved. I soon learned that Mitch's grandfather had died two years before, and that he had recently appeared in Mitch's room in the form of a purple ball," as I wrote in an article. "Vitamin Pills for Schizophrenics," in the April, 1974 issue of *Psychology Today*.

The parents told me that Mitch's talks with his grandfather were relatively harmless when considering some of his other bizarre behavior. Sometimes he ate 60 candy bars a day, most of them stolen from neighborhood stores. He set fires in his room; he attacked his sisters.

"I did not know exactly what was wrong with Mitch, but I thought it probably had a chemical basis, and that it was connected to his almost insatiable appetite for sweets," I wrote.

Following a battery of lab tests, the results showed a normal EEG. The blood tests revealed no sign of liver, kidney or thy-

47

roid disease. An analysis of his hair indicated satisfactory levels of a number of metals and minerals; the amounts of vitamin B12 and folic acid, another B vitamin, were within the normal range. His glucose tolerance curve was the only indication of what was wrong. He was hypoglycemic. The level of sugar in his blood decreased when he ate carbohydrates, leaving him with too little sugar to nourish his nervous system. Hypoglycemia patients, like Mitch, are often overweight and undernourished.

After breaking the news to Mitch's parents, assuring them that both the hypoglycemia and schizophrenia were treatable, I put Mitch on a high protein–low carbohydrate diet with small meals and frequent in-between meal protein snacks. This diet is described in greater detail in another chapter.

After each meal Mitch took 500 milligrams of vitamin B3 (niacin), 500 mg. of ascorbic acid (vitamin C), 100 mg. of pyridoxine (vitamin B6), 100 mg. of pantothenic acid (another B vitamin), 200 I.U. of vitamin E, and a multiple B complex tablet. These doses are very large for a child, but, since all of these vitamins—except vitamin E—are water-soluble, his body could easily break them down and eliminate them as waste if he had taken more than he could use.

Mitch began to respond almost immediately. Within the first week he became calm and was able to concentrate. I increased the niacin dosage to 1,000 mg. after each meal. I had purposely started him on a lower dose because niacin can cause flushing of the skin and itching. But the larger doses made him nauseous, which is also a common problem. I see it in about 20 per cent of my patients. I switched him to niacinamide, another form of vitamin B3, and the nausea subsided. After one month, Mitch began to lose weight and his schoolwork improved. I increased his vitamin C intake to 1,000 mg. three times a day. He continued to improve, although he still disrupted his class from time to time and argued with his parents. I supplemented his diet with L-glutamine, an amino acid that appears to benefit brain nutrition.

"During our three-month interview, Mitch's parents told me that he was doing very well," I continued in the article. "None of his perceptual distortions had recurred. He was still losing weight. His ability to concentrate continued to improve. Only two problems remained. He became weak if he did not eat, a common symptom of hypoglycemia. And he continued to wet his bed, a persistent behavior his parents had not mentioned while he was exhibiting his more extraordinary symptoms.

"Mitch and his vitamins are going to be together for a long time. If his symptoms do not reappear, he will continue his present treatment for several years. Then I will reduce the doses slowly to see if he can function normally with less vitamins," I said.

Although Mitch's case is not a classic case of depression, it serves to illustrate the problems that hypoglycemia (low blood sugar) can cause. "I'm tired all the time," patients tell me. "Everything is an effort for me." "No matter how much I sleep, I wake up tired." "I feel terrible but my doctor says that nothing is wrong with me."

These are some of the complaints I hear when a patient has low blood sugar. Of course, not everyone with these common complaints has low blood sugar, but this is a condition which is frequently overlooked in the usual diagnostic check-up. For some obscure reasons, which I am unable to understand, a number of physicians refuse to admit that there is such a thing as hypoglycemia. They call it a "fad disease." How much needless suffering could be relieved but goes on because some physicians will not consider alternatives? Many patients have told me, "My doctor wouldn't test me because he says there is no such thing as hypoglycemia."

Hypoglycemia is not new. The early recognition of hypoglycemia did not meet with the general neglect by the medical profession which it now suffers. In the 1920s, shortly after insulin, the hormone that is involved with the utilization of sugar, was discovered, Dr. Seale Harris made some interesting observations. When a person was given too much insulin, the sugar in the blood would go to a low level and many symptoms would occur until sugar was provided. The person would feel weak, cold, clammy, nervous, shaky and, in some instances, more serious effects—fainting and convulsions.

Dr. Harris observed that some of his patients, who were not on insulin, had the same appearance and symptoms that would be expected if they had been given too much insulin. He confirmed his suspicions by testing the blood sugar and finding that, when symptoms were present, the blood sugar was low. Symptoms in these cases were relieved within a matter of minutes by eating sugar or having an injection of a sugar solution.

FIG. 1: A normal configuration. In addition to having normal sugar levels throughout, the patient does not experience any symptoms, such as tiredness, irritability, tremendous hunger, headache, sweating or rapid pulse.

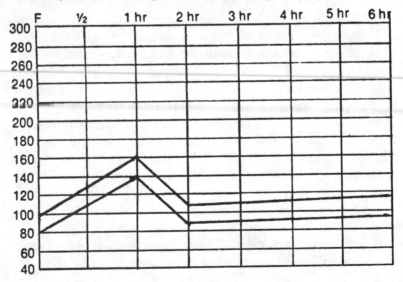

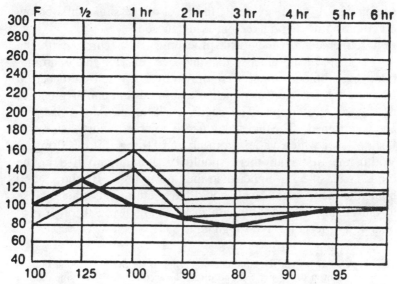

FIG. 2: A flat curve showing a failure of response of the blood sugar rising 50% above the fasting level within the first hour. Fasting level is 100; the highest point within the first hour is 125 mg.%, giving a total rise of only 25 mg.%.

In looking for a treatment, he found that the blood sugar went low after eating sugar. In those who have this condition, the eventual response in the body when sugar is eaten is to *lower* blood sugar. Dr. Harris developed a high-protein, low-sugar diet with frequent feedings that is still the basic treatment for hypoglycemia. The American Medical Association awarded Dr. Seale Harris special recognition for his work, which, as often happens in medicine, was promptly forgotten by all but a few physicians.

Hypoglycemia is often considered by the more astute diagnosticians when their patient's severe symptoms of weakness, dizziness or fainting apparently have no other medical basis. The doctors draw blood samples to test the sugar level when

51

symptoms are most severe. If the level of the sugar falls below a certain point, hypoglycemia is diagnosed.

A refinement of diagnostic procedure has occurred with the development of the glucose tolerance test. During this examination, several blood samples are drawn over a 5- to 6-hour period after the patient has consumed a measured amount of glucose, usually a sweet drink. The sugar levels of the blood samples are determined. The normal glucose tolerance curve shows a fasting level which varies from around 80 mg.% to 100 mg.% Within the first hour there should be a minimum rise in the blood sugar of 50% higher than the fasting level. By the second hour, the blood sugar level should have returned to a level close to the fasting level and remain in that range even through a 6-hour test. (See Fig. 1 through Fig. 5)

FIG. 3: A relative hypoglycemic curve. Fasting is 89 mg.%. Second hour is 58 mg.%, a drop of 31 mg.%. The drop was accompanied by symptoms of loss of color and fatigue and nervousness. This is called a relative hypoglycemia.

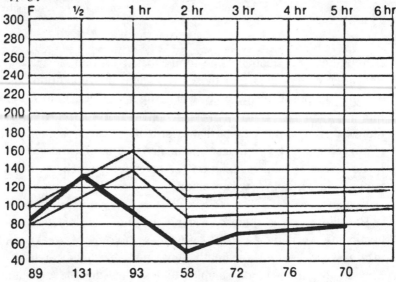

MAYBE YOU HAVE HYPOGLYCEMIA?

In making the diagnosis of hypoglycemia, too often the results are scrutinized for one level that falls below some predetermined point which has been designated as normal. In my experience using this criterion, over 90 per cent of treatable hypoglycemia will be missed. And it seems that, the more hypoglycemia is considered a fad, the lower the blood sugar must fall in the estimation of some physicians before they will make a diagnosis of hypoglycemia.

Not too many years ago, if one of the sugar levels in a 5-hour glucose tolerance test was below 60 mg.% (60 milligrams of glucose in 100 cc's of blood), the diagnosis of hypoglycemia was made. There are many who will not make a diagnosis unless the level falls below 50 mg.%. Recently some research was published that suggested that 50 mg.% is too high, since studies showed that healthy men, after fasting for three days,

FIG. 4: A typical sawtooth curve with a double peak, the first being at the half hour, the second being at the second hour.

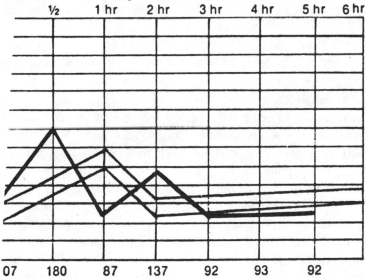

½	1 hr	2 hr	3 hr	4 hr	5 hr	6 hr

07   180   87   137   92   93   92

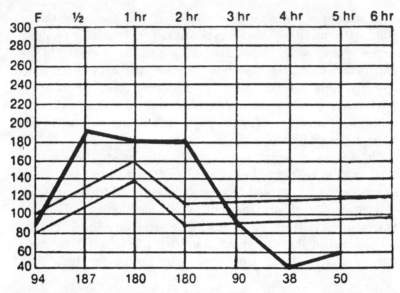

FIG. 5: This figure shows several abnormalities. One is a pre-diabetic state with the rise of blood sugar to 187, failure to return to the fasting state the second hour, and then showing a reactive hypoglycemia with the blood sugar below 40 at the fourth hour.

could reach a level of 30 mg.% with no ill effects. Some researchers are determined to prove that there is no such thing as low blood sugar.

Attempting to set a point above which you are normal and below which you are abnormal is artificial and obviously not based on reality. Such artificial levels may be true for a percentage of the population, but that is of little significance to any one individual. For example, take an arbitrary figure of, say 90% of those individuals whose blood sugar falls below 50 mg.% will be hypoglycemic. The question arises, at what point did the hypoglycemic symptoms begin to appear? Did all the symptoms appear at 50 mg.% and none at 51 mg.%? In how many people did symptoms appear at 60 mg.%? How many at

MAYBE YOU HAVE HYPOGLYCEMIA?

70 mg.%? So you see, taking one figure as the criteria and diagnosing by the lab report is artificial and unfair to the patient, who is seeking expert advice in order to get well.

Dr. H. Saltzer recognized these problems when he developed the concept of relative hypoglycemia. In doing 5- and 6-hour glucose tolerance tests, he recognized that many people who develop definite symptoms of hypoglycemia through the test—weakness, sleepiness, faintness, rapid pulse, sweating, irritability—did not have a blood sugar fall to a point which would meet the criterion for making a diagnosis. Yet the observations were undeniable. These patients were developing hypoglycemic symptoms. He began to realize that what was normal for one person might be abnormal for another, and it may be in the hypoglycemia range for that person.

From his work he developed criteria that would apply to these cases, whose levels failed to fall below a specified point, yet they had symptoms during the test. Specifically, he took the fasting level of the blood sugar as the "normal" level for that individual. The fasting specimen is one that is taken when there has been nothing to eat or drink for 12 hours prior to testing. Two criteria were developed by Dr. Saltzer: 1) If any of the blood sugar levels fall more than 20 mg.% below the fasting level, and the hypoglycemic symptoms are present, the patient is diagnosed as a relative hypoglycemic. 2) If there is a fall of 50 mg.% or more in any one hour, accompanied by symptoms, a diagnosis of relative hypoglycemia should be made.

In addition to these criteria, there are two abnormal graphs which are also hypoglycemic types. 1) A flat curve. The normal glucose tolerance graph shows a rise of the blood glucose within the first hour of 50% more than the fasting specimen. A failure to achieve that level results in a more or less flat appearance of the glucose tolerance curve when the figures are plotted on a graph, hence, "the flat curve." 2) In a normal glucose curve,

55

the second hour specimen and the subsequent specimens are within a short range of the fasting specimen. In some tests, a significant rise of glucose is noted after the second hour, which creates a second peak in the plotted glucose curve. This type of configuration is called a sawtooth curve and is a hypoglycemic curve.

In summary, the glucose tolerance test may result in the diagnosis of hypoglycemia if: 1) Any level falls below a specified level, usually 50 mg.%, but may be lower depending on who is doing the interpretation. 2) If any glucose level is 20 mg.% below the fasting level and accompanied by symptoms. 3) If there is a fall in any one hour of at least 50 mg.% and accompanied by symptoms. 4) If there is failure of the blood sugar to rise 50% (not 50 mg.%) above the fasting blood sugar level (flat curve). 5) If there is a significant rise in blood sugar after the second hour, forming a second peak (sawtooth curve).

Until this point the diagnosis has been based mainly on the glucose tolerance test. Sometimes the glucose tolerance test is not sufficient to make the diagnosis. The patient's experiences through the test must be weighed very heavily in determining the diagnosis. A glucose tolerance test that shows no abnormalities in the results of the blood sugars is only normal if the subject remains without any symptoms throughout the test.

Sometimes I have seen test results that were normal, but the patient felt terrible throughout the testing and/or a few days following the test. Some of the symptoms that have been mentioned are tiredness, headache, irritability, hunger, depression, weakness, fainting, pallor and sweating. When the history is obtained of having such experiences during the testing, there is enough evidence to presume the presence of hypoglycemia. When treated, the results are often gratifying.

This type of presumption is justified when one realizes that the testing is done at hourly intervals. I have seen tests done at half-hour intervals, where the blood sugar reached a low

MAYBE YOU HAVE HYPOGLYCEMIA?

point at a half-hour and resumed to the normal level at the regular hourly interval. In these tests, if only hourly samples had been obtained, the results would have appeared normal and hypoglycemia would have been missed if the diagnosis was made on the basis of laboratory findings only. The ideal way to conduct tests is with an experienced technician who is able to recognize symptoms and draw blood sugars at that time, rather than at a predetermined, specified time. The body is not always cooperative in giving the results looked for at the time when the blood sample is drawn in the usual manner of testing.

Before having a 5- or 6-hour test ordered, however, there should be a consultation with a physician to determine whether or not the symptoms for which the physician is being consulted are related to hypoglycemia.

Dr. S. Gyland studied several hundred patients with low blood sugar. He listed the frequency of symptoms as follows:

Nervousness–94%.

Irritability–89%.

Exhaustion–87%.

Faintness, dizziness, tremor, cold sweats, hot flashes–86%.

Depression–77%.

Vertigo, dizziness–73%.

Drowsiness–72%.

Headaches–71%.

Digestive disturbances–69%.

Forgetfulness–67%.

Insomnia–62%.

Worrying and anxiety–62%.

Mental confusion–57%.

Internal trembling = 57%

Palpitation of the heart and rapid pulse–54%.

Muscle pains–53%.

Numbness–51%.

Indecisiveness–50%.

HYPOGLYCEMIA

Among the other symptoms which occurred in less than 50% of his patients were the following:

Unsocial, asocial, anti-social behavior, crying spells, lack of sex drive, allergies, incoordination, leg cramps, lack of concentration, blurred vision, twitching and jerking of muscles, itching and crawling sensations of skin, gasping for breath, smothering spells, staggering, sighing and yawning, impotence in males, unconsciousness, night terrors and nightmares, rheumatoid arthritis, phobias, fears, neurodermatitis, suicidal intent, nervous breakdown, convulsions.

In making a diagnosis, naturally not all of these symptoms must be present, but certainly some of the more common ones should be significant enough to be mentioned. Also, most of the time there is a history of a craving or heavy intake of sugar, starch or alcohol. If tremors or spells of weakness are prominent symptoms, these may be relieved by eating something sweet or starch, and this is good presumptive evidence of hypoglycemia. All symptoms cannot be relieved by eating carbohydrates, as advised by an editorial in the *Journal of the American Medical Association*.

Because depression is so common in those with hypoglycemia, any person who is depressed without a clear cut obvious cause for that depression should be suspected of having low blood sugar. As we noted in Dr. Gyland's studies, 77 per cent of his patients with hypoglycemia complained of depression.

CHAPTER 8

The Hypoglycemic Diet

AFTER THE DIAGNOSIS OF HYPOGLYCEMIA is made, treatment can begin. Often there is confusion in thinking about the treatment. If there is a low blood sugar, the obvious response would be to eat more sugar. Fortunately, that advice is not given much any more, because eating sugar is what makes the blood sugar level go low. The dietary suggestions, as outlined in this chapter, are directed at preventing the low level from occurring. As I have indicated, there are three aspects of the diet which must be strictly followed or there will be only a poor response at best. The three elements are: 1) High protein–low carbohydrate diet; 2) Small meals; 3) Frequent high-protein snacks.

1) *The foods that you eat.* This should be a high-protein, low-carbohydrate diet. By low-carbohydrate I mean the absolute absence of all processed carbohydrates (sugar and white flour). I also instruct my patients not to use any artificial sweeteners or honey while on this diet. Some fruits and vegetables are very high in carbohydrates and so they are restricted. Caffeine in food or drugs may cause a release of the stored body sugars, therefore, all caffeine products are restricted. I should point out that many products have added sugar, so anyone on this diet must diligently read all labels.

59

2) *The amount of food.* This varies with individual tastes. You should eat enough so that you are not hungry, yet you should not overeat.

3) *When you eat.* The best way to explain why frequent snacks are necessary is to observe the glucose tolerance test curve. The object of the diet is not to let the blood sugar fall, so this can be overcome by having a high-protein snack prior to the time the blood sugar falls on the glucose tolerance curve.

A printed diet is obviously not ideal for every patient, since individual requirements vary. But this is the type of diet that has worked successfully for most people. Some people may need more carbohydrate than is allowed on the diet; some people may need less. I give each patient the printed diet as a guideline, then modify it a bit at subsequent meetings if that becomes necessary.

When reading different books outlining diets for the treatment of hypoglycemia, the reader will quickly observe many diverse opinions. One doctor may allow apples, another advises avoiding milk, a third suggests staying away from artificial sweeteners. Although confusing, a quick analysis shows that the differences are more superficial than basic. The majority of the writers agree on the three basic principles of the diet: 1) low carbohydrate, high protein; 2) small, but adequate amounts of food at any one time; 3) regular meals with frequent snacks. The apparent differences come with an attempt to define low carbohydrate for everyone, a task that is almost impossible. As a result there are some fruits and vegetables which are found on some lists as acceptable and on other lists in the to-be-avoided category.

Each treating nutritionist has a diet with which he or she is familiar and is able to modify for the individual as treatment progresses.

The only departure from the usual low carbohdyrate–high protein diet is one advocated by Paavo Airola, Ph.D. in his

THE HYPOGLYCEMIC DIET

book *Hypoglycemia: a Better Approach*, suggesting the use of a high complex carbohydrate–low protein diet. In my experience this program is effective in some cases, but not successful as often as the customary high protein–low carbohydrate diet. My guess is that the failures on the high complex carbohydrate diet are due to the high incidence of grain sensitivities in our population. The diet is a possibility, however, when treating strict vegetarians.

Many people are now nutritionally aware and question the high amount of protein in the suggested diet. They are correct in their observation, but the diet is suggested as a Treatment Diet for about four months and then changed to a Maintenance Diet during which time a more ideal program of less protein and more carbohydrates may be used.

Those who may have a significantly high cholesterol level should not be on a diet with large amounts of cholesterol. Each person should, of course, consult their own physician before attempting any dietary changes.

The Treatment Diet
ALLOWABLE FOODS

Meats: Any meat, fish, sea food, fowl. It is best to stay away from processed luncheon meats because of the additives and high salt and fat content.

Liquids: Vegetable juices, decaffeinated coffee, decaffeinated teas, all waters, carbonated or not.

Nuts and seeds: Convenient as snacks, and may be used in recipes. Beware of high caloric content due to fat.

Grains: All whole grains. Don't use processed or enriched grains, which are primarily carbohydrate. If not sensitive or allergic, try to consume about two cups of cooked grains daily, divided between two or three meals.

Pasta: Whole-grain pastas may be used as one serving of

61

whole grain. The whole-grain pastas tend to have a strong flavor and require a hearty sauce.

Bread: Whole-grain bread only. Be careful to look for the "Whole-grain" label. Sometimes "whole-wheat" breads are little more than colored, white enriched flour. Bread should be limited to two slices a day not eaten at the same sitting. Sandwich lovers may try a whole-grain pita and make a pocket sandwich.

Dairy and eggs: Preferably low- or nonfat. Yogurt is allowable, but not sweetened with added fruit. Eggs are OK. Limit milk to two 8 oz. glasses daily, not consumed at one sitting.

Vegetables: Preferably fresh and steamed or raw. Low-carbohydrate, allowable vegetables:

beet greens	radishes	okra
celery	watercress	onions
chicory	asparagus	peppers
Chinese cabbage	bamboo shoots	peas
chives	bean sprouts	beans
cucumbers	broccoli	spinach
endive	cabbage	squash
escarole	cauliflower	tomato
fennel	collard greens	turnip
lettuce	eggplant	zucchini
olives	leeks	
parsley	mushrooms	

Fruits: Limit fruits to two servings a day because of the sugar content. Don't eat more than one serving at one sitting, and always consume fruit as part of a meal, not as a snack by itself.

cantaloupe	coconut	lemon/lime
rhubarb	cranberries	gooseberries
strawberries	muskmelon	casaba melon
boysenberries		

THE HYPOGLYCEMIC DIET

FOODS TO AVOID

All foods containing sugar. Read label and be aware of the several different ways in which sugars are described, e.g. all words ending with *ose*—fructose, glucose, sucrose, etc. They are also listed as "natural sweeteners," all syrups. READ LABELS CAREFULLY.

All "enriched flours." These are primarily carbohydrates.

All "quick cooking grains." These are primarily carbohydrates.

Artificial sweeteners. Avoiding the sweeteners added to food allows the taste buds to regain their natural sensitivity to sweetness, and after about six weeks added sweeteners are too sweet. At that point it is easy to stay away from sugar without feeling deprived.

Honey. Even though it is "natural," it is much too high in carbohydrates for those with hypoglycemia.

Caffeine. Caffeine plays havoc with blood sugar levels.

Alcohol. Alcohol slows down a natural process which takes place in the body converting available protein to needed sugars.

How much to eat.

Eat enough to avoid hunger, but not so much that you feel stuffed. The amounts to eat obviously vary from person to person.

When to eat.

Three small meals should be eaten as well as frequent protein snacks. The frequency of the snack is determined by the glucose tolerance curve. For example, if there is a drop of the blood sugar at the third hour, snacks will be suggested every two hours. The object of the snack is to provide insurance against the blood sugar falling to hypoglycemic levels even if all the correct foods have been eaten. Even without the advantage of information from the glucose tolerance test, most people would be safe snacking at a frequency of every two hours. The snack is taken two hours after last eating and continued till bedtime.

63

Food may be consumed more frequently, but not less frequently.

Suggested snacks.
A small portion of meat, dairy products, nuts or seeds, whole grain bakery products. If weight is gained, dairy products and nuts and seeds should be limited because of the high caloric content. Two tablespoons of a liquid flavored protein, available in some health food stores, is a good snack where weight is a problem. However the liquid protein may be used only as a snack, not as a substitute for a regular meal.

Cheating and Getting Away with It
During my years of treating hypoglycemia, I have found that expecting 100 percent adherence to the diet is unrealistic most of the time. My observations are that a little cheating several times a week prevents any positive changes.

However, if the diet is strictly followed for six days, the seventh day may be completely free and full of "junk" food without compromising the expected beneficial results. The first two weeks following a junk day program, nothing much seems to happen. But from about the third week and on, a deviation including a lot of refined carbohydrates and or alcohol usually results in a reaction which always lasts one day and most often starts the next day, but may have its onset two or even three days after the junk day. The reaction is one of feeling tired, irritable and generally not well. If the junk day additions have been adding only desired fruits or vegetables, there may be no bad reaction.

For most people having a reaction a couple of times is enough to be convinced that they are better off not eating the foods which caused them to feel so bad. At that point the diet is usually regarded as something to be desired rather than something which represents deprivation. Under those circumstances the diet becomes easier to stay on.

What to Expect During the Treatment

In staying on the diet, there are usually three distinct phases noted during the course of treatment. The stages last from three to five weeks each in most instances, although I have seen some patients go through each stage at weekly intervals, while others took two to three months for each stage. Most people are in each stage about one month. Granted this routine can be tedious, but it eventually pays off in improved mental health, loss of weight and a general well being in the majority of my patients. Therefore, it is well worth the trouble. One must be patient and not expect overnight results. While it is human to go off the diet temporarily, in order to insure success, one must follow the diet religiously. The satisfaction of feeling better is the ultimate reward.

First stage. The first stage is characterized by not feeling well. Weakness, dizziness, mild nausea and depression may be increased during this stage, especially if the diet represents a radical departure from the foods usually eaten.

When a patient is placed on the hypoglycemia diet, I give him a printed instruction sheet to follow. Included on the sheet is a list of foods which must absolutely be avoided. If the patient says spontaneously, "Why those are the foods I eat all the time," I know that the first month will be difficult. Also, if the patient has been accustomed to eating lots of sugar, I expect some difficult moments, because all sugar, except for some fresh fruit and juices, has been eliminated from his diet. The more sugar that the patient has normally eaten, the worse he will feel during the first stage.

It is important to warn the patient that he may have trouble adjusting to the new diet. But, in order to cure the depression, it is imperative that the hypoglycemia diet be followed. Nor-

65

mally, there is a craving for sugar and starch during the first three weeks. As the patient becomes adjusted to the high-protein diet, however, he usually finds that the craving disappears.

Sometimes patients will call and say, "Doctor, I know you said I'd feel bad, but I didn't think you meant this bad." If there is a significant weakness or deterioration in the patient's condition, I increase their fruits from one to two servings a day. The slow transition from a high- to a low-carbohydrate diet is usually enough to relieve some of the more distressing symptoms during the first stage.

The danger during this first stage is that the patient will feel so weak and uncomfortable, without realizing that this is a normal reaction, that he may abandon the diet. I have to reassure him that the craving for sweets will diminish if he continues the diet. If the diet is broken frequently, however, the craving may continue indefinitely.

Second stage. If the patient has made it through the first stage—and most of them do because they are motivated by the desire for health—the second stage begins after three to five weeks. It brings its own rewards, disappointments and dangers.

The beginning of the second stage is abrupt; the sense of well being is sudden and obvious. Energy abounds, depression lifts, no anxieties are to be found, pains have disappeared and, in general, there is a relief from symptoms and a feeling of being cured. The truth is that this wonderful relief means that the patient is not yet out of the woods. But any relief is welcome after such despondency. While the second stage is ushered in dramatically with a feeling of getting well, there are rapidly changing forces still at work. One day or part of the day may be super good, followed for no apparent reason by days as black as they ever were. These up-and-down days are a crucial stage for the patient, and again I have to reassure him that this apparent setback is only temporary.

As the second stage progresses, the ups become less dramatic and the downs less fearsome, finally reaching a more constant level in about the same time that the first stage took. But, in order to avoid misinterpreting the good days as a cure and the bad days as a hopeless situation, the patient and family must be told what is to be expected, what these changes mean, and why a solution is just around the corner. If the patient thinks, "I'm never going to get well," it will only contribute to his depression. I find that these uncomfortable and gloomy feelings can be pushed aside if the patient has adequate warning and knows what to do about it. I usually emphasize that this roller coaster feeling means that progress has been made and that the patient is now entering a new stage towards getting well.

The patient should be instructed to live one day at a time and to cope with the up or down day as best he can. When there is a good day, enjoy it by doing something that is fun. But don't make plans for tomorrow. When the patient feels energetic, there is a natural tendency to make plans. This can be particularly frustrating if the plans, perhaps involving friends and family who have been neglected, come during one of the down periods. Those who have been depressed, low in energy and self-esteem, don't need any more failures. Therefore, living one day at a time is the best policy during this period. If there is a bad day, relax as best one can and think positively. The day will pass and tomorrow will be better.

Third stage. The beginning of the second stage is dramatic. The beginning of the third stage is sneaky. As the second stage progresses with less variation in mood and energy, there comes a point where the patient, having calmed down from the merry-go-round, up-and-down days, says: "You know, I'm better than I was before I started this diet, but I'm still not as well as I want to be." Although he is obviously better, the improvement is not sufficient to enable him to carry out his ordinary responsibilities to family, work and friends. Some patients are disappointed at the beginning of the third stage because they think

67

of the dramatic sense of well being experienced at the beginning of the second stage which is no longer present. They feel they have regressed whereas they actually are better than they were before starting their program but not well enough to function satisfactorily.

The third stage is characterized by a gradual improvement in energy. In fact, the improvement is often so gradual and natural that it is hardly noticeable to the patient. The patient must recognize the changes that have taken place to add encouragement to stay on their diet. A recognition is usually accomplished in those who say they are the same by reviewing their complaints before treatment started.

Of course, most patients are aware of the change that takes place during the third stage. They report the improvement in energy levels, ability to cope with day-to-day living, disappearance of nervousness, better sleeping habits and absence of depression. The symptoms they had before treatment began usually begin to disappear during this third stage. And they can handle ordinary problems that used to be impossible.

During this stage the need for psychotherapy is usually evaluated. The patient often gives me a clue that he is progressing nicely by saying something like, "It's absolutely incredible. I have the same situation that I couldn't cope with before but now it doesn't bother me at all. I simply handle the situation as it arises, like everybody else. I don't make a mountain out of a mole hill like I used to." Consequently, these patients see no need to enter into psychotherapy because they are handling their problems in a sensible manner.

On the other hand, some people may say, "I certainly feel better physically and I have more energy, but I'm still not up to solving some of my problems." At this point, I usually recommend psychotherapy. The therapy is meaningful and effective at this time because the patient becomes a participant in psychotherapy.

THE HYPOGLYCEMIC DIET

In order for psychotherapy to be successful, the patient must bring: 1) A mind capable of identifying problems, thinking of possible solutions, and judging the appropriateness of those solutions. 2) A body that is healthy and energetic enough to implement the solution judged appropriate. A patient with hypoglycemia after successful dietary treatment has these tools to bring to psychotherapy, and together with motivation, psychotherapy can be meaningful, effective and relatively short-term. Without the clear head and healthy body, the sessions often deteriorate into relentless complaints and a rehash of symptoms. Many patients who find out that they have low blood sugar while they are in psychotherapy go on to correct their diet and start to show meaningful progress in psychotherapy after being on a plateau for long periods of time.

The main danger during the third stage is the lack of recognition of the gradual changes. Some patients automatically expect the dramatic changes that came with the second stage. Another danger is the premature abandonment of the diet by some who feel so good that they see no need for it, or by those who become bored with the diet after having been on it for over two months. Merv Griffin often tells his TV audience how he overcame hypoglycemia, and I remember his saying on one telecast that if he even has a glass of wine his old symptoms of hypoglycemia quickly return. Instead of becoming bored with the hypoglycemia diet, one must learn to serve the acceptable foods in various ways. Start by getting one of the cookbooks at your health food store and learning new ways to cook the foods that are allowed.

Fourth stage. If the patient has been through each of the three stages as outlined, with each stage lasting three to five weeks in most cases, I advise staying on the strict diet for another three to five weeks. The purpose of this extra time is to have the patient get used to the feeling of good health. Some patients begin to recognize changes that were never expected

69

because they accepted some problems as "normal" without knowing that a problem existed. One middle-aged woman was surprised at how clear her thinking was after three months on the diet. She reported that she could make decisions and her mind worked quickly and without confusion. She had accepted the slow thinking, confused state and inability to make decisions as just a sign of "old age." Another woman was surprised at her clear thinking; a new experience for her. In retrospect, she had always been slow in her thinking, but accepted it as normal.

THE MAINTENANCE DIET PROGRAM

The diet during the initial four months is strict and can get monotonous. I tell the patients at the outset that the strict diet is for a minimum of four months and will be varied later. As I mentioned, some people may have to continue on the hypoglycemia diet indefinitely, but, once the hypoglycemia has been arrested, some alterations can be made. For example, some of the forbidden fruits and vegetables might be taken in small amounts from time to time (potatoes, corn, bananas, plums, apples, etc.)

One weakness for good nutrition in the strict diet prescribed is the paucity of whole grains. When expanding the diet, I prefer to add grains, followed by natural fruits and vegetables, since some of the high-carbohydrate fruits and vegetables were a no-no during the first four months. If the patient tolerates these additions, he can experiment with varying the snack times. The last addition is to occasionally have something with sugar—if they must—during special occasions, such as holidays, dinner parties or eating in a special restaurant. During this phase of determining how expansive the individual's diet can become, there are many guidelines to be followed:

1) Timing of the foods to be added.

Most people assume that, if they eat something that doesn't agree with them, the reaction will come within a few hours.

THE HYPOGLYCEMIC DIET

This is false. The reaction follows by one day, sometimes two days, and in a few cases three days. So, to be on the safe side, the new foods should not be tried closer together than every three days.

2) Most people eventually observe that their body is not static and, to their surprise, they may expand their diet at one time with no unpleasant effects. At another time, the slightest variation from the strict original diet produces a profound reaction.

The key to when to add food and when not to is stress, which can be thought of as an emotional or physical stress. During times of stress the body is supersensitive to any variation from the strict diet. Physical stress may be the slightest infection, such as a cold or sore throat, erratic sleep for a few nights, overwork, etc. Emotional stress may be arguments or worry about a variety of things. By stress I do not mean the everyday problems that everyone faces in life, but extra ones that occur from time to time.

Sometimes the individual is not even aware of the added stress, but the body usually has an awareness and a unique system of warning the individual who is hypoglycemic. For this person, who has been treated for hypoglycemia, there is a clear sign of the presence of stress if a craving for sugar returns after it has been absent for some time. This craving is usually a good indication that stress is present. It is imperative that the patient continues with the hypoglycemic diet at this time. He should also attempt to find out the cause of the stress in order to avoid further problems. It is at this time that I may increase the intake of vitamin C and the B complex, since these water-soluble vitamins are known for their anti-stress qualities.

Knowing the body's sensitivity to sugar under stressful situations, it is prudent for anyone with hypoglycemia to prepare themselves prior to and during stressful situations. This is done by adhering to the hypoglycemia diet and taking the necessary

71

HYPOGLYCEMIA

food supplements, if they have been prescribed. In addition to illness, which is unpredictable (a sudden cold, for example), other stressful events which might arise for the housewife include entertaining friends, house guests, ill children, the increased demands of the preschool months, etc. Students usually find exams stressful. Businessmen have to cope with changing business conditions or unexpected business trips which may be demanding. It is not too difficult for each of us to predict an upcoming stressful situation. Again, the hypoglycemic diet should be strictly followed in order to get through the tense period.

Perhaps the most dramatic examples that I have seen of how the body is not static have occurred with some of the patients who have reported their experience on vacations, especially ocean cruises. Usually they will try different foods from the wide assortment, since they are in a totally relaxed and carefree state. They notice no immediate adverse effects from either the foods or alcoholic beverages. It is truly a time to eat, drink and be merry. Being convinced that they are cured, the patient returns home to find the ordinary problems—bills, the hot water heater is on the fritz, there is trouble with the family car, etc. Assuming that his hypoglycemia is cured, he resumes his former high-carbohydrate diet, and, after about two weeks of this indiscretion, the patient feels in need of hospitalization because most of the original symptoms have returned.

At this point it doesn't take much persuasion to convince the patient that he must continue the hypoglycemia diet. Usually at that point good results can be observed in two to four weeks. During the relaxed atmosphere of the voyage, the body was able to handle the insult of sugar. But under the everyday stresses, the body rebelled with disabling symptoms.

The biggest mistake that patients make during the phase of going off the hypoglycemia diet and adding new foods is not paying attention to how their body is reacting to the new diet.

72

THE HYPOGLYCEMIC DIET

If a food doesn't agree with them (for example, they may have added a high-starch food like potatoes or a high-sugar food like dates), these symptoms might occur: tiredness, lack of interest, depression, anxiety, headache, backache, etc. In other words, their old symptoms may recur. Of course, the symptoms may not return as dramatically as they exited during the treatment period. Just as in the third stage when there is a gradual improvement, there may be a gradual deterioration so subtle that the patient hardly notices it. One day is not quite as good as the day before. There is apprehension that things may not be as good as they have been. If these feelings are not taken into consideration and the situation is not looked at objectively, the patient's condition may deteriorate rapidly. Patients are cautioned to pay attention to how they feel and what their bodies tell them. Under the circumstances I may be forced to suggest that they adhere to the strict diet for another few months. Or, as I have explained, they may have to remain on the diet, with slight modifications, for the rest of their life. This high protein–low carbohydrate diet is not as catastrophic as one might think, since there are endless ways to create appetizing meals with meat, fish, eggs, cheese, milk, yogurt, the acceptable fruits and vegetables, etc. Thousands and thousands of people are adhering to this diet with no appreciable inconveniences. Their reward is sparkling good health and boundless energy. Wouldn't you say it's worth the trouble? Most people are able to expand their diet except when under physical or mental stress, sometimes a stress as minor as a sore throat. It is rare to find a person who must always stay on the strict treatment diet in order to function successfully.

About 80 per cent of the improvement takes place during the first three to four months. This improvement is due to the biochemical changes related directly to the dietary and vitamin program. I have also noted that, after six to twelve months following the initial improvement, there is usually further im-

73

provement. This is marked by a calmness, self-pride and assurance that is psychological in origin.

Because most people with hypoglycemia have been ill for many years before treatment has started, a defeated, hopeless attitude has been present. It is an attitude based on reality because they actually have felt bad. The patient had not been able to cope with life successfully. Relationships would break down because of depression, irritability, lack of energy. Careers, plans for the future and special projects would follow the same unsuccessful course. All of these failures only reinforced the patient's self-contempt of worthlessness. In order to build confidence and pride, there must be a series of successes which follow the maintenance of good health. As the patient becomes more confident (his golf game improves, a hobby turns out to be profitable, he graduates with honors from college, he marries his childhood sweetheart, he finds a totally rewarding job, he can get along with people, etc.), he begins to progress by leaps and bounds. Of course, these successes must not be short-lived; they must be of sufficient duration to let the patient know that he is well at last and that his triumphs will not suddenly be snatched away.

During this period, which is usually six to twelve months after the initial improvement, the extra 20 per cent of psychological improvement occurs. At this point the patient is usually able to cope. Usually, if a problem arises, the patient is so mentally and physically alert, he can solve the difficulty by himself. It is the ability to handle life's problems through the operation of a keen mind and healthy body that leads to the eventual return of self confidence and a feeling of emotional strength.

CHAPTER 9

Case Histories with a Happy Ending

Georgette: This 27-year-old married woman came to my office complaining, "I've had something wrong with me all my life." She had had numerous therapies (psychotherapy, pharmacotherapy) until she found out that she had hypoglycemia. A few weeks prior to her visit she had attempted suicide.

Her complaints were being tired and depressed all the time. "I'm unable to work and I don't want to get out of bed," she told me. Because of her symptoms she became very insecure and had lost her self-confidence; at times she felt the situation was absolutely hopeless. She also complained that things seemed unreal.

Before seeing me she had worked intermittently in computer sales or as a secretary, but she was unable to take the pressure of a job. She was divorced and, prior to her illness, she was supporting herself and her child. There was a family history of her mother being depressed. She had attempted to follow the hypoglycemic diet but she did not eat the high-protein snacks that were called for. The only noticeable physical complaint was a lowered blood pressure.

Because of the sensory distortions which she complained of,

75

I placed her on large doses of vitamins three times a day. This consisted of four niacin tablets (500 mg.), four vitamin C (500 mg.), one pyridoxine (200 mg.), one pantothenic acid (100 mg.), one vitamin E (400 I.U.) and a B complex capsule (50 mg.). A hair test revealed some deficiencies of minerals, so I prescribed manganese (50 mg. three times a day), potassium (50 mg. three times a day), and an iron supplement, once a day. I also placed her on a tranquilizer, which she stopped on her own after three weeks. and, of course, she was instructed to follow the prescribed diet.

She was seen at approximately monthly intervals, and, after the first three weeks, she began to feel better, less depressed. After two months she told me that she was definitely much better and able to think more clearly. By three months she said, "At last I feel normal. My thinking is as good or better than it has ever been."

Because of the steady improvement, she went back to work. There were two subsequent relapses, both in stressful situations. One was when she failed to follow the diet and vitamin program; the other was when she had some serious disagreements with her husband. Both of these events required a short hospitalization, during which time she quickly recovered. At the last admission she requested further psychotherapy and this was arranged through consultation. She has continued to be well since then.

Carol: A married woman and a schoolteacher, this 24-year-old patient worked as a teacher in the first grade and had a known history of hypoglycemia: fainting spells, depression, irritability, easy confusion and a physical complaint of cold hands. Both her brother and father were hypoglycemics.

She was immediately started on a hypoglycemic diet with vitamin supplements after breakfast and dinner: a B complex tablet (100 mg.), three vitamin C (500 mg.), one vitamin E

(400 I.U.). After the results of her hair test were returned, she was placed on manganese (50 mg.) and potassium (50 mg.) twice a day. After one month on the diet she noted that, if she did not have her frequent snacks, she became very involved in a compulsive activity.

Her glucose tolerance showed a severe drop with the first hour and she had been told that she must have snacks at least hourly. Another complaint was frequent colds, which lasted four to five days. She had been taking an antihistamine, which she was able to stop until she developed the flu. This was quite a departure from the chronic upper respiratory infections that she was subject to.

It is interesting to note that she had stopped eating sugar when she first found out she was hypoglycemic, but her improvement in health came only after she increased the frequency of the snacks and added vitamins. After two months on the program, she reported that she did not have the cold hands and her mood and energy had improved.

She stated that previously she had been "really down" and worrying unnecessarily about things that weren't worth worrying about and blaming herself for things that weren't really her fault. At the end of three months, she had none of the original complaints and was feeling fine. She did develop a minor symptom, that of itchy palms, which was unexplained. Other than that she was a different person.

Charles: A 25-year-old single male, who worked as a grocery clerk, complained: "I feel very depressed but I don't know what triggers it. I don't want to be alone. I don't have any interest in anything." His energy level ranged from "exhausted" to "hyperactive." Not surprisingly, he was a heavy user of refined carbohydrates.

The glucose tolerance test showed a flat curve with a drop at the third hour, accompanied by dizziness, headache and

77

weakness. He was started on a hypoglycemic diet, an antidepressant and these vitamins twice a day: B complex (100 mg.),
two vitamin C (500 mg. each), and one vitamin E (400 I.U.).

He had some personal problems which neither of us felt were
directly related to his symptoms. It was thought, however, that
he might eventually need psychotherapy, but I suggested that
we not initiate therapy until he was well into the hypoglycemic
regimen, some three to four months hence. After the first month
he sometimes felt bad but the shaking that he originally had
had stopped. He was also able to realize that he had created
some problems with his parents where none really existed.

During the second month, after going off the diet a couple
of times, he developed a headache and tired easily. He had,
however, been able to work a 48-hour week without any depression. By the end of the second month he felt that he didn't
have any problems and that his over-all health and energy had
leveled off. He did not believe that the therapy was necessary
because he was very active and doing a lot of interesting things.

I saw him approximately six weeks later. The antidepressants
had been reduced, he was not having any headaches, and he
was even considering leaving his job for one that was more
challenging than a grocery clerk. About five months later he
telephoned to say that he had gone off his diet for about five
weeks and the shakiness and depression had returned. He agreed
in the telephone conversation to go back on his diet, and there
have been no more serious complications.

Fred: This 23-year-old single male came to my office complaining that he started using heroin again. He had a mild addiction and had been using heroin intermittently over a few years.
He had been on parole for heroin addiction following a voluntary self-committal. A few years later he started using it again.
He complained of being very depressed, he had no interest in
anything and there was some anxiety. His appetite was poor

and he used the drugs to relieve his tensions. He knew of no reason for the depression.

He did tell me that he remembered being depressed when he was six years old, and, in the third grade, he was taken to see a child psychologist. In the family history there was a paternal uncle who was a suspicious paranoid who eventually committed suicide. The paternal grandmother had diabetes. The maternal grandmother was depressive and used morphine for her arthritis; she was always sick and negative.

His diet consisted mainly of hamburgers, beer and refined carbohydrates. I recommended some general lab tests—liver studies, thyroid, blood counts, urinalysis and glucose tolerance test (GTT). The tests were within the normal limits, except the GTT, which showed a relative hypoglycemia with fasting of 88 mg.% and the two hours 54 mg.%, showing a 34 mg.% drop at the second hour from the fasting level.

I recommended a hypoglycemic diet and these vitamins three times a day: niacin (1 gram), vitamin C (1 gram), pyridoxine (100 mg.), pantothenic acid (200 mg.), vitamin E (400 I.U.), and B complex (50 mg.). He was followed at monthly intervals and, after the first month, he began to improve. He had not returned to heroin, although he occasionally used marijuana and drank a little beer. He was seen again in a couple of weeks. His energy remained up but his beer consumption had been reduced. He told me that he would hit a low spot for no apparent reason. But he began to feel a control over his depression.

Two weeks later he was feeling "very good." He was getting along well with people, he was staying close to his diet, and he had moved away from home to be on his own. Three weeks later his family reviewed his history and we all agreed that he had made remarkable progress.

A little later I increased his diet to include more fruits and vegetables. The following month he stopped the niacin for a few days and immediately felt bad. He was seen throughout the year at approximately monthly intervals and he continued to do well.

About one year after being on the program, I discovered an abnormal liver condition and the vitamins were stopped while he underwent extensive examinations at a university center. The conclusion was that he had a disease of his muscles which had been present for a long time and it was unrelated to the vitamin intake. After being off the vitamin program for about nine months, he telephoned requesting to start again because he had been feeling "physically and mentally better on the vitamins."

After resuming the vitamins, he noticed that for the first few weeks he remained rather depressed and "run down." But his energy gradually increased, he was sleeping well and had more confidence. In fact, he decided to take an extensive trip.

Michael: This 19-year-old boy complained that he was easily depressed and on the verge of suicide. He was unable to keep a job because he felt that his employer was making too many demands on him, so he would either leave or be fired. He had used marijuana rather regularly; two suicidal attempts had been made some years ago with medication.

His mother reported that he would swing in and out of depression frequently, sometimes during the same day. There had been no abnormal elations. He had maintained the same pattern since childhood and had been in many difficulties with the law as a teenager. His family was upper middle-class.

As a child he had wet the bed until he was 10 years old, he complained of multiple fears, and he was always known to give up easily. He did visit a psychiatrist when he was younger. It was noted that he had a high I.Q., but, during the seventh grade, his grades went from A's to D's. As a child there had been such diagnoses as minimal brain damage and hypochondria.

When I first saw him he had been in psychotherapy for 2½

years "but the pattern had not changed." In the family the great-grandmother had had a serious diabetic condition. His mother was nervous and had her "ups and downs." The glucose tolerance test was done and it showed a flat curve. In addition to the dietary and vitamin program, I felt he needed a great deal of supportive therapy, so weekly interviews were scheduled for about five months. Then the frequency became monthly rather than weekly.

Originally he had been placed on the following vitamins three times a day: niacin (1 gram), vitamin C (1 gram), pyridoxine (100 mg.), pantothenic acid (100 mg.), vitamin E (400 I.U.) and a B complex (50 mg.). To this I added thiamine, (1 gram), and later these minerals: manganese (50 mg.) twice a day, potassium (50 mg.) twice a day. A slow improvement was noted during the time he was beginning the treatment; he had started school and had been working fairly steadily during that period.

At the end of five months, I felt that he had reached a maximum improvement on the supportive type of therapy. He was no longer depressed and he had begun meaningful activities at school and work. Even so, I felt that he would benefit from a more intensive type of treatment and he was referred for transactional analysis. I continued to see him at monthly intervals and he generally did very well as long as he stayed on his hypoglycemic diet and vitamin program. During the first five months of this treatment, I had prescribed anti-depressants, which were later discontinued. He is continuing in school and has been doing very well. His vitamins have been decreased to twice a day and he is continuing to benefit from his transactional analysis.

Robin: This 21-year-old single female student had a history of depression on and off for three years. When I first saw her, she told me about her lack of confidence, hopelessness, and a suicide attempt two years previously with over-the-counter medications. She had undergone psychiatry, psychotherapy and drug programs in the past. Her mother reported that Robin walked around the house aimlessly and sat on her bed and stared. She tired easily and had headaches. She had been adopted as an infant.

Her dietary history showed that she consumed a large amount of refined carbohydrates. Her glucose tolerance curve was flat, so she was started on a hypoglycemic diet and these vitamins twice a day: B complex (50 mg.); vitamin C (1 gram); vitamin E (400 I.U.), thiamine (1 gram) and an anti-depressant. During the early weeks, she had difficulty staying on the diet and there were no improvements; she felt "tired and spaced."

After the first monthly visit, when I found that she had difficulty staying with the program, I scheduled an appointment for her two weeks later. She was observed to be in an "up and down mood." She was still expressing feelings of hopelessness: "I don't see how I can ever get out of this rut. I don't think I will ever change."

She then came back a month later and had maintained the diet and vitamin program, she had started to work, liked her job and began feeling well and enjoying life. Her brother commented, "Man, she's a different person." During this time she had gone off her diet when she was with other young people, which caused her to be tearful, frightened, tired.

A month later she had been in a serious accident but her mood remained optimistic, without any evidence of depression. Her energy remained high. She was occasionally dizzy and remained well except for a slight case of nausea. Other than that she has progressed nicely.

Casper: This 18-year-old boy had multiple complaints—periods of slow thinking, trouble waking up, usually dopey, always tired, bad memory, "sick to my stomach," below normal temperature, poor grades, losing interest after an hour, inability to

82

concentrate. His mother stated that he had been excitable all his life, he was slow to speak, he had a high I.Q. but never did well in school. He had been given Ritalin to speed him up in high school and it worked for a while. But the Ritalin had been stopped because of chest pain. Multiple checkups failed to discover a reason for his tiredness. A glucose tolerance test revealed a relative hypoglycemia based on a fasting blood sugar of 89 mg.% and a three-hour of 58 mg.%.

He was started on these vitamins twice a day: B complex (50 mg.), vitamin E (400 units), pantothenic acid (100 mg.), vitamin C (1 gram), along with the hypoglycemic diet. Within the first month he began to show some improvement; his energy improved so that he was able to mow the lawn. His mother told me that he had not had any headaches for three weeks, although he had had frequent headaches since he was 10 years old. He was seen at monthly intervals, there was a gradual increase in his social activities, and he was able to get along at home, especially with his brother.

After overeating on Thanksgiving, he noticed that he was extremely tired. Appointments were then made at six- to eight-week intervals. He continued to improve, including his ability to concentrate, but his memory became a problem. His mother said that, whenever he ate something that he shouldn't, he became headachy and "dopey." He resisted the idea of psychotherapy at first, feeling that his only problem was a disagreement with his parents about his appearance and the neatness of his room.

It took about eight months for Casper's thinking to clear. It didn't take him as long to make decisions, and he was very busy with hobbies. Scheduled meetings were made at two- to three-month intervals. The only problem which remained was a lack of social involvement. There was no evidence of depression. He remains well, except for mood changes and irritability when he eats sugar. His school work has improved to all B's and A's. I now see him at three-month intervals.

Cecil was a 34-year-old bachelor who complained of physical and mental disabilities and had gone to a physician for symptomatic treatment. The physician had prescribed Valium and sleeping pills. He told me that he felt physically terrible, a feeling of heaviness, tired, exhaustion. "I can't seem to get through the day, even after I have slept well."

Two years before he started feeling depressed. He quit his job and went back to graduate school, but the depressed symptoms soon appeared again. He had some shakiness, pains in his back, a feeling of not wanting to be around people, irritability, and a conscious effort of having to control his temper and actions all the time. "Life seems aimless and no fun any more," he said.

His general health was good and there was no diagnosis of diabetes in the family. His diet consisted of coffee in the morning with two teaspoons of sugar; he would have either three cups of coffee or tea with sugar, a hamburger and a Coke for lunch, and dinner would be steak or chicken with a salad and milk. Snacks were apples and bananas. He was taking some vitamins, a B complex, minerals and vitamin E before he came to the office.

A glucose tolerance test was done, which showed a flat curve and he was instructed to request extra blood samples from the lab if he had any symptoms. He did develop a symptom of extreme tiredness at 2½ hours and a blood sample taken at that time showed a drop to 60 mg.%. Fasting was 81 mg.%.

He was started on the hypoglycemic diet and these vitamins three times a day: B complex (100 mg.), vitamin E (400 units); vitamin C (1 gram), and two dolomite (calcium and magnesium) tablets. He was seen one month after starting the diet, at which time he reported that he felt horrible the first week, much better the second week. He still did not have much energy but his depression was improved. His sleep had also improved. He decided to move to another city and so I did not see him for 2½ months. He reported that he was "going great, feeling fabulous."

During his absence, he stated that he was slowly getting more energy, but that he no longer had severe depression and headaches. he was much more enthusiastic about his work and had not been taking any medication other than the vitamins.

He was seen approximately six weeks later. He had been sticking to his diet and he felt well, his energy was good and he had entered graduate school where his studies were progressing satisfactorily. His vitamins had been decreased after about three months to once a day, and I told him that, unless something unforeseen developed, I saw no reason for him to make any more appointments.

Jane: This 31-year-old single woman has a high-priced job in the fashion field. She complained of being tired, depressed, lack of energy, frequently angry at the world. She remembered similar feelings in grammar school. Before her appointment she felt as if she would faint, she had a numb feeling in her right hand, her vision was poor. She reported that she had no more personal problems than most people; her general health was good. Because she was a Christian Scientist, she usually didn't go to doctors.

Although she was not overweight, she had been following the Weight Watchers Diet for about four years. On the day prior to the time she almost fainted, she had had several candy bars, cocktails and starchy foods. There was a periodic craving for sweets. The glucose tolerance test revealed a relative hypoglycemia: fasting, 102 mg.%; four hours, 62 mg.%; and a drop from 152 mg.% the first hour to 76 mg.% the second hour.

She was started on a hypoglycemic diet and these vitamins

85

twice a day: B complex (50 mg.) vitamin E (400 units); vitamin C (1 gram). Appointments were scheduled at monthly intervals. Following the first month she continued to have trouble with tiredness and an inability to sleep. During the second month, some days were good and some were bad, including one entire week which was very difficult for her. She continued to feel tired during the following month, but she began to realize that she was ''more in touch with what was happening around her.''

She was very good about staying on her diet and taking her vitamins. She did have some periods of feeling extremely anxious and ''wound up.'' During this time there were a lot of changes taking place in her life that she had to cope with. In the following month she felt happy and experienced no feelings of depression. She was beginning to understand the stressful things that affected her badly, such as lack of sleep and her pattern of overextending herself with activities when she felt well.

After another month she continued to feel well and noted that, whereas she used to force herself to do things because she was depressed, she no longer had that compunction. I arranged to see her every two months and she continued to function at a very high level, even handling several difficult problems that had cropped up in her life. By now she was aware of which foods to avoid and continued to be well. Check-ups are now infrequent.

Barney, a 46-year-old married business man, loudly announced, ''I'm an alcoholic.'' He was a sporadic drinker who gradually drank more and more and then was unable to stop. He had been treated with Antabuse and group therapy. AA never appealed to him. He would stop drinking for one and a half to two weeks, rarely longer. Both his business and family responsibilities were suffering because of his drinking. He had the D.T.s a few times, gout and a gastric ulcer.

There was no family history of alcoholism and he had no cravings for sweets. It was noted that he did not think properly, his creativity was fuzzy and his concentration was poor. He felt that perhaps he used alcohol to slow himself down because he would get into a frenzy of activity and be unable to stop. A glucose tolerance test showed an elevated one-hour specimen with a rapid drop between the first and second hour.

I prescribed a hypoglycemic diet and large doses of these vitamins: niacin (500 mg.), vitamin C (1 gram), pyridoxine (200 mg.), pantothenic acid (200 mg.), vitamin E (400 I.U.), a B complex (100 mg.), L-glutamine (400 mg.) three times a day; and riboflavin (vitamin B2) (100 mg.) and thiamine (500 mg.) once a day. In about a month he was noted to have improvement in his mood, and, while his energy was at a very high level, he was able to slow himself down when he wanted to.

He continued to show improvement and was followed at monthly intervals. After about five months the vitamins were simplified to a B complex twice a day, vitamin E (400 units) twice a day, L-glutamine (400 mg.) twice a day and vitamin C (1 gram) twice a day. He continued to take Antabuse. His business and family relationships improved and he was sufficiently well to weather some very difficult business problems. I saw no reason for him to need further therapy.

Bernard, a 27-year-old separated, unemployed man, reported that he had been hyperactive as a youngster. At the time of his visit he had not been working for a year and a half because of lack of interest and no energy. He had stopped school six credits short of a master's degree. He had been a moderate user of marijuana and LSD.

He was aware of his depression. Five years previously he

had had hepatitis twice, but otherwise his general health was within normal limits. His diet included a lot of coffee and toast. The glucose tolerance test showed a fasting specimen of 91 mg.%; three-hour specimen, 58 mg.%, therefore, a diagnosis of relative hypoglycemia was made.

I suggested the hypoglycemia diet, along with the following vitamins twice a day: niacin (1 gram), vitamin C (1 gram), pyridoxine (200 mg.), pantothenic acid (100 mg.), vitamin E (400 units), B complex (50 mg.) and a multi-mineral tablet. As most of my readers know, niacin is vitamin B3, pyridoxine is vitamin B6, and pantothenic acid is another B vitamin. I prescribe these individual B vitamins because of the extra strengths needed. The full B complex tablet is also essential to give the patient folic acid, vitamin B1, vitamin B2, etc.

Within the first month he stated that he felt like doing more, he was not depressed but more alert. He had begun to lose weight, which he had wanted to do (this is an added dividend of the high-protein, low-carbohydrate diet), and, except for a little difficulty with sleeping and occasional outbursts of anger, he felt particularly well. In fact, he immediately began looking for a job.

David was a challenge. An alcoholic who looked older than his 58 years, he had many complaints, accompanied by his lack of hope and trust that his problems could be resolved. He was irritable, he would fly into rages at home and he had constant migraine headaches related to his tenseness. He had taken a lot of Darvon. His main complaint was hostility, tremulousness and depression, and his general attitude was: "Why bother to work? Why bother to do anything?" After every argument with his wife, he felt that he should get a divorce and give up everything. He had gone into psychotherapy but never followed through with it.

A workup revealed a relative hypoglycemia, the abnormalities being a drop between the first and second hour of almost

100 points, and a drop of 22 points below his fasting level at the third hour. He was seen for a second interview to discuss the findings. During this interview he became extremely irritable because he felt that I did not have all of the material to present to him immediately as he walked into my office. He also stated, "I realize you don't like me."

One month later, after starting the vitamins twice a day: (B complex (100 mg.), vitamin C (1 gram), vitamin E (400 units), folic acid (50 mg.), manganese (50 mg.), potassium (50 mg.), and a small amount of thyroid (even though his thyroid tests were normal), he came in and said: "I feel better than I have ever felt in my life. I feel like I usually felt when I took Darvon to feel good."

However, during the first two weeks after starting the diet, he complained of headaches and being tired all the time. The third week after being on the diet he was not taking any Darvon or other medication. The pattern over the next month was somewhat the same as the first two weeks, difficult times followed by an improvement during the last two weeks.

The following month after he had been on the diet for a total of three months, his wife said, "Well, your disposition is a hell of a lot better." He noticed that he had more stamina and felt like exercising, which was something he had not done in many years. During the month he had only been irritable on two occasions.

In about three months, David had a marked improvement from his irritability, aggressiveness. He seemed wary of his improvement and afraid that his old self would return. I find this rather common, as I have mentioned in this book, and it usually takes another six to twelve months to gain the self-confidence and self-respect which their new improvement brings them.

CHAPTER 10

Hypoglycemia: Questions and Answers

AFTER MANY YEARS of treating hypoglycemia, and an equal number of years lecturing about hypoglycemia, many recurring questions have been asked by those with hypoglycemia. Those questions and my answers to them are as follows.

When can I stop the diet?

Although modifications of the diet may and should be made after improvement has been achieved, usually after about four months' treatment, those with hypoglycemia are never able to eat refined carbohydrates on a regular basis without experiencing a return of symptoms. Hypoglycemia is not cured, it is controlled. Hypoglycemia is like arsenic poisoning. The symptoms will stop eventually after stopping the arsenic, but if the arsenic is started again the symptoms return. The same is true of hypoglycemia. Stay with your program, the symptoms will lessen. Start sugars (refined carbohydrates) and the symptoms will return.

Why can't I have artificial sweeteners?

In addition to the accumulating evidence suggesting that artificial sweeteners may not be the best thing for your health, there are other good reasons for those with low blood sugar to stay away from them. After avoiding added sweetness for six weeks, the taste buds become very sensitive to sweet flavors. At that time sugar usually tastes too sweet. Some of my patients have even reported that a fresh fruit, such as pineapple, was too sweet.

Since the optimum, long-term diet requires the avoidance of refined carbohydrates, the diet is much easier to follow once the taste buds no longer find sweetness desirable.

Can a natural sweetener like fructose be used?

Fructose, like artificial sweeteners, will not cause a hypoglycemic response, but the same problem exists with fructose as with the other sweeteners; you never give your taste buds the opportunity to change and become more sensitive to the sweetness of foods. So like the artificial sweeteners, you may avoid the hypoglycemic reaction, but you will have a struggle avoiding refined carbohydrates, because they will still be desirable.

Another potential problem with fructose is that no one really knows what would happen if people started to eat as much fructose as they eat sugar, now at approximately 125 lbs. per person in the United States.

I thought honey was O.K., because it is natural

Forget it! Honey is a concentrated carbohydrate, and any concentrated carbohydrate will stress the body's ability to control the sugar level in the blood. Even natural fruit becomes a culprit when several servings are consumed in one day.

Are hypoglycemia and diabetes opposite?

They are opposite only in the sense that hypoglycemia means there is a low level of sugar in the blood, and diabetes means

91

there is a high level. However, more importantly, they both are disorders in the ability of the endocrine system to regulate blood carbohydrate levels properly, and untreated hypoglycemia often progresses to become diabetes.

The symptoms from each extreme of this improper regulation are also quite different. Diabetes may begin with almost imperceptible symptoms, but can progress to very serious symptoms. Hypoglycemia may have pronounced symptoms, but they are only life threatening if the person becomes so despondent that suicide becomes a serious consideration.

If I cheat on the diet, do I go back to Stage One and start all over again?

It depends on how much and how often you are off the diet. If you have paid no attention to the diet for several weeks, you may have to start all over again. If the dietary lapses are once a week or less, then you haven't impaired your chances of getting well. Many times I have advised those just starting a dietary program to stay on the diet strictly for six days and indulge with all the carbohydrates they want on the seventh day. The first two weeks on the diet usually are not accompanied by any further symptoms when the diet is broken, but from the third week on a definite cause and effect is noted. The effect of going off the diet, with a lot of carbohydrates on the seventh day, is usually a day of fatigue, depression and return of symptoms. The reaction never lasts more than 24 hours, usually starting the next day, but sometimes beginning the second or third day after the diet has been broken.

My purpose in advising this type of "torture" is that most people will stay with the diet for a longer period if they know they can be off of it from time to time. For example, rather than saying to oneself, "I can never have a dish of ice cream," they say, "I can have whatever I want one day a week, as long as I stay on the diet strictly the other days."

HYPOGLYCEMIA: QUESTIONS AND ANSWERS

Another reason for advising breaking the diet once a week, which has never interfered with anyone's progress, is that after two or three bad reactions most people tend to stay with the diet strictly and have no desire to eat anything which will produce a feeling of illness. After establishing the relationship between heavy carbohydrate consumption and a state of illness, there is no longer a feeling of deprivation in avoiding past food favorites.

I have hypoglycemia. Are my children going to be affected?
Diabetes and hypoglycemia do affect several members of the same family, but just because a parent has a glucose problem doesn't mean that the children have inherited an air-tight guarantee to have the same problem. It is prudent to be aware of the development of possible problems. The best plan of attack is preventive. Help the children develop good eating habits at an early age, the earlier the better and easier to do.

When should I repeat the glucose tolerance test to find out how I'm doing?
Probably never if you have remained fairly faithful to the diet. Progress is measured by evaluating change of symptoms, not by repeating a tortuous test. If the diet has not been followed for a few years or longer, symptoms are present and someone wants to start over again, there may be some reason to repeat the test. The main reason for doing a glucose test at that time is to determine if there is any suggestion of diabetes. Before a glucose tolerance test is done there are other laboratory tests, easier on the patient, which may be done to determine the presence of diabetes.

I have read that the glucose tolerance test is not accurate because it is not normal to eat as much sugar as is given to the person being tested. Also aren't you really testing a corn al-

93

lergy when you use corn sugar as a challenging dose during a glucose tolerance test?

There are many controversies involving the accuracy and significance of the test. In spite of those objections to the test, I have found it of great value in the diagnosis and treatment of hypoglycemia. Many people need some laboratory confirmation of suspected disorders. Generally most people have more determination to stay with a program, which is at times difficult, if they have some objective proof, like a laboratory report, which confirms the diagnosis.

The test might also be helpful in tailoring a program for the individual. An important part of the program is the frequency of eating. For most people a two-hour snack between meals is sufficient, and that is because most people with hypoglycemia have a drop in blood sugar between three to five hours on the test. It is important to snack before the blood sugar drops. If the drop occurs at the second hour after eating, or even before, then snacking every two hours is not sufficient and improvement is in jeopardy.

The test may be important in determining prognosis. In a flat or sawtooth curve there may be a doubling of the time it usually takes to show a response. You only know the type of curve by doing the test. Without the knowledge of the presence of one of those abnormal curves, treatment might be stopped prematurely.

Do I have to stop smoking?

There is ample evidence to prove that smoking is not good for anyone's health. Even so, I do not advise trying to stop smoking at the same time the diet is started. Demanding too much at first can easily discourage anyone from doing anything. A step at a time is better. It may seem slower, but in the long run the task gets done.

The proper time to tackle the problem of quitting tobacco is when the diet has become second nature and there is a definite change in mood. Usually all these criteria are met by the end of the second month on the diet. At that time, it is not unusual for me to hear that the person recognizes that they don't feel as well after smoking. That observation and experience becomes a powerful motivator.

Isn't exercise good?

It's terrific, but only when you have the energy to do it, which is not the case with most people who start a hypoglycemic diet. Exercise should be done only when the body tells you to do it, not when your mind thinks it is probably a good idea. Now of course, I'm talking about those with hypoglycemia, not those with terminal laziness or a malignant aversion to exercise. That's another problem. Again, about the end of the second month, the body starts sending messages "move me, stretch me." That's the time to start, but carefully. Only do enough to feel better at the end of the exercise than you did before starting. If you do too much and it takes anywhere from several hours to a few days to recuperate, then you probably are being counterproductive with your exercise program.

I don't want to eat meats. How can I go on a hypoglycemic diet?

Most people who ask this question mean red meats. When I refer to meat I'm talking about animal protein, fish and fowl in addition to red meats. It is not necessary to eat red meats, but it is desirable to eat animal protein for the purposes of this diet. Lacto-ova-vegetarians will do well if they are careful to eat all the necessary amino acids (protein building blocks) in the correct proportion. The advantage of eating animal protein is that the animal protein already has the proper proportion of the amino acids needed. Anyone who doesn't eat animal protein must be aware of the sources of the amino acids in order to get all of the essential ones in the proper proportion. By follow-

95

ing the recipes in the classic *Recipes for a Small Planet* the necessary mixture will be achieved.

I'm gaining weight on this diet. What can I do?

When weight is gained on this diet, which does happen, but rarely, the most common cause is the use of cheeses and/or nuts as the snack food. Both of those foods are high in calories due to the high fat content. It is easy to add up extra calories quickly. One acceptable solution is to use a flavored liquid protein as the necessary snack. You cannot use the liquid protein as a substitute for a meal, but it functions well as a snack. The liquid protein may be difficult to find in health food stores, since it fell out of favor a number of years ago after causing many health problems to dieters who used it as their only food for several weeks at a time. It remains a valuable snack for some hypoglycemics and it is still available.

I'm losing too much weight on this diet. What can I do?

This complaint is more frequently heard than problems with gaining weight. Usually weight is lost because junk foods carrying all the extra calories in the refined carbohydrates and fats are avoided. The body starts to work towards its optimum weight when on an optimum diet.

Weight does not continue to be lost indefinitely. After the initial weight loss, the weight usually stabilizes. If more weight is desired, more calories may be eaten by increasing portions or by using more nuts and cheese with their relatively high caloric content. Another method to gain weight is by exercise which should be started when the body is ready. Bulk and muscles may be added by a program of body building with heavy weights.

I eat out a lot. How can I stay on the diet?

With a little advanced planning, knowing your diet and

knowing your restaurants, there should be no problem in eating out all the time. It may be difficult to go into a fast food restaurant with a limited menu, but fast food restaurants aren't the only restaurants available.

There may be another problem if you don't have control of your own diet or restaurant choice when dining out. This might happen if you are the guest at a dinner in someone's home, attend a banquet or meetings when you are not able to choose your own menu. These problems may also be overcome with a little planning. If you know the hosts well enough to discuss your dietary needs, do so. Most people will be very cooperative. If you are hesitant to discuss your needs, for whatever reason, then one way to stay on your diet is to eat before you are trapped at a dinner with nothing to eat. Later when served your dinner, pick out those foods which are on your diet and push the remaining food around the plate, as most children have done, especially a child served vegetables, almost any vegetables.

Don't panic, or deprive yourself of social or business contacts. Going off the diet once a week won't cause any setbacks.

I'm going in for an operation. How can I stay on the diet?

If you have a physician to whom you can talk, and you should have, ask for plain saline instead of glucose and water whenever intravenous fluids are necessary. Ask to be placed on a hypoglycemic diet, or if that is a problem ask for a diabetic diet which is probably easier for the dietician and kitchen. Hospitals seem to do a better job in providing a diabetic diet than a hypoglycemic diet, which is often interpreted, in my experience, in a bizarre fashion in many hospitals.

But, remember, if you need medical attention and your diet has to be sacrificed for a while, so be it. Don't worry about it. You must take care of first things first, and when you are in control again, get back on the diet.

97

PART 3

Other Medical Causes of Depression

CHAPTER 11

Viruses and Depression

VIRAL DISEASES have been around a long time, but it was
not until the 1980s when viruses and the diseases they cause
commanded the attention of all members of the thinking public
and the efforts of scientists around the world. Acquired immune
deficiency syndrome (AIDS), an illness which is caused by a
virus infecting the immune system, has been in the media almost daily for several years. Other viruses have also been discovered, and, although not fatal, they are expensive in terms
of human suffering.

Of particular interest to those with depression is the Epstein-
Barr virus. Many years ago there was a complex of symptoms
called infectious mononucleosis and labeled the "kissing disease" for the way it was transmitted. It seemed, at that time,
to affect young people of college age and was often found
spreading through college campuses. The symptoms were flu-
like, low-grade fever, muscular aches and pains, headache and
fatigue, which was often pronounced. The disease complex was
also characterized by the long time the symptoms lasted. The
more discouraging part was that even if the person felt better
for a while, the symptoms returned. It was not unusual to have
recurring episodes of illness for two to three years.

101

OTHER MEDICAL CAUSES OF DEPRESSION

Some time later, the virus causing infectious mononucleosis was discovered by two British scientists for whom the virus is named. It is now known that the infectious mononucleosis symptom complex may be only a forerunner to a longer debilitating illness now known as Epstein-Barr virus syndrome.

In the mid-1980s tests became available commercially which allowed the laboratory diagnoses of this illness. Once exposed to the virus, the body retains certain antibodies which can be picked up by testing. Other antibodies are present when the old disease is reawakened, making differentiation possible between old and recurrent disease. Through the use of these tests it has been estimated that over 50% of the adult population has been exposed to the Epstein-Barr virus sometime in their lives. Since most people do not go on to develop a chronic Epstein-Barr illness, we can assume that the body has some good defenses against this virus.

Using the test to determine the presence and activity of the virus changed some physicians' minds about the diagnosis given to some of their patients. The chronicity of the illness, the variety of symptoms consisting of generally not feeling well, aches and pains, sometimes swollen glands, all found in the setting of a patient who is depressed, has fooled many physicians into assuming the problem is psychological and the physical symptoms are psychosomatic.

In the past, before chronic Epstein-Barr virus syndrome was recognized, a lot of the patients made the pilgrimage from physician to physician, and after years of being told that all laboratory findings were normal, dutifully, at the suggestion of their physician, sought out psychiatric help, which was of limited value. As in all cases of depression, the cause must be determined before proper, effective treatment is successfully administered.

June, a divorced woman in her 50s, was one of those people who made the medical rounds. She had been depressed for

years and, in spite of antidepressant medication and psychotherapy, she remained depressed. She found the psychotherapy interesting because of the insights she gained about herself, which
she felt were valid, and later, when she was feeling well she
was able to use. But at the time of therapy she was mostly
discouraged because she was not feeling better. After changing
therapists again, during the initial interview by her new psychologist, she was surprised when asked questions about her health.
The psychologist learned that June not only had complaints
about feeling depressed, but also experienced a profound fatigue. There were sometimes days in a row when she was unable to get out of bed except to attend to the basic human
needs, and other days when ordinary chores seemed equated
easily with the effort it would have taken to climb a mountain
peak. The depression and recurrent fatigue broke up her mar-
riage when her husband could no longer tolerate what he called
her laziness. He felt his perceptions were validated when several
psychiatrists characterized her problems as psychosomatic. Her
new psychologist learned she also had muscle aches and pains,
and flu-like symptoms. None of these symptoms had, in the
past, responded to the antibiotics prescribed and, in spite of all
her care, she continued to have episodes of weakness, feelings
of physical illness and depression. Her new psychologist suggested the possibility of a viral illness and referred her to a
medical specialist who made the diagnosis of chronic Epstein-
Barr virus based on the history obtained and the laboratory
findings.

There is no accepted, proven treatment for this condition at
this time, but making the diagnosis was the best psychotherapy
June could have had. It strengthened her to know that she really
wasn't crazy and that when she kept insisting through the years
that "something is wrong" she was correct and the psychosomatic diagnosis was incorrect. She has shown improvement
over the past few years and that may be in large part due to

the beneficial effect of the knowledge that there is a reason for the way she felt all those years and that reason was not something elusive and in her head.

Epstein-Barr does seem to affect more women than men, but anyone might develop this illness. Perhaps the most interesting question is why more people are not chronically ill, since so many people have evidence of previous exposure to the virus. The answer is undoubtedly in the functioning of the immune system, about which more is being learned rapidly, in part due to the desire and need to conquer the virus causing AIDS. It has been common experience that the symptoms of Epstein-Barr become manifest at times when the immune system is debilitated by other illnesses.

Since there is no known treatment which has proven to be highly effective, the best treatment at this time seems directed towards strengthening the immune system. In general terms, a good diet, adequate sleep and exercise, such as rapid walking when possible, are immune system strengtheners. The addition of nutritional supplements may prove useful. Vitamin injections have been advocated by some, but the effectiveness of many of the treatments advocated are awaiting more studies.

Part of the treatment directed towards strengthening the immune system must include good attitudes. In the past several years many studies have shown the effect of attitude on the immune system. In the past, before there were scientific terms to describe the mental attitude-immune system connection, people would talk about the will to live bringing people through catastrophic illnesses. June's improvement did coincide with her change of attitude following the diagnosis.

Chronic Epstein-Barr virus syndrome is but another example of the necessity to make a careful diagnosis of the cause of depression before successful treatment is given.

Chronic Fatigue Syndrome (CFS)
For the past several years a hot debate has been progressing

in the medical community about the very existence of a disease called Chronic Fatigue Syndrome. Some medical investigators claim that there is no such thing.

The symptoms are characterized by months of profound fatigue, usually associated with a recurrent sore throat, low-grade fever, muscular aches, headaches, gastrointestinal symptoms and tender lymph nodes. The evidence, in my opinion, is overwhelmingly in favor of a disease process involving the immune system and not "psychological" as some investigators claim.

At one point the symptoms were thought to be related to the Epstein-Barr virus, but studies over the past few years point to a more complicated, less easily determined cause than the Epstein-Barr virus or other known viruses.

Whereas CFS had been dismissed as "hypochondriasis" a few years ago, the symptom complex is now gaining more attention and respect from physicians and investigators. In the Science Section of the New York Times, December 4, 1990, the lead article was *Chronic Fatigue Syndrome Finally Gets Some Respect*. Several theories were outlined as possible avenues of investigation which are ongoing.

Treatment at present remains nonspecific, that is, taking good care of oneself from a medical, nutritional and psychological view point. Many studies of the use of specific medications are being done, but no treatment has as yet emerged as the final answer.

One of the most comforting treatments is in the knowledge that the person with CSF really has a disease and isn't going crazy. A large organization, The CFIDS Association, Inc., has been formed, providing support, research, information and a referral service. The Association answers the needs of interested physicians and the public. The group has chosen instead of Chronic Fatigue Syndrome the name Chronic Fatigue and Immune Dysfunction Syndrome (CFIDS), and in March 1991

began publication of *The CFIDS Chronicle, Journal of the Chronic Fatigue and Immune Dysfunction Syndrome Association.*
For more information the national organization may be reached at:

The CFIDS Association, Inc.
P.O. Box 220398
Charlotte, NC 28222-0398
704 362-2343
704 365-9755 (FAX)
1-800 442-3437

CHAPTER 12

Yeast Infections and Depression

THANKS TO C. Orian Truss, M.D., a physician practicing in
Birmingham, Alabama, another physical cause for depression
has been uncovered. Over twenty years ago he was treating a
woman for severe migraine headaches and incapacitating premenstrual tension. When she complained, incidentally, of a
chronic vaginal infection due to yeast and it was treated, he
was surprised to find that the migraine headache also improved.
In addition she reported that she was no longer bothered by
premenstrual tension. This clinical observation started Dr. Truss
on a course of investigating the connection between chronic
yeast infection, called moniliasis or candidiasis, and symptoms
affecting his patients physically and psychologically.

After several years of further observations on other patients,
he presented his first paper, "Tissue Injury Induced by Candida
Albicans," to the Eighth Annual Scientific Symposium of the
Academy of Orthomolecular Psychiatry, held in Toronto in
1977. Subsequently the paper was printed in *The Journal of
Orthomolecular Psychiatry,* Volume 7, Number 1. Further papers were presented to the same group and papers published in
the same journal, but it was not until 1983, when *The Missing*

OTHER MEDICAL CAUSES OF DEPRESSION

Diagnosis by C. Orian Truss, M.D. (available in paperback and hardcover from *The Missing Diagnosis,* P.O. Box 26508, Birmingham, AL 35226) was self published, that some physicians and a larger portion of the suffering public began to take notice. Other books from other authors followed, magazine articles appeared, television appearances were made and yeast infections and their many manifestations became a matter of public knowledge. As with all new observations, some elements of the medical community prefer to distrust early observations and wait for twenty to thirty years to accept ideas which are then old news. Then there is the group of practitioners who embrace every new idea as the last word and answer to all of humankinds' ills, until the next new discovery. As always the truth belongs somewhere in between, but the concepts should not be made to suffer, and diagnosis and treatment should not be denied because of the excesses of either side of the medical community.

What exactly is candidiasis? Firstly, some physicians have misunderstood this condition to mean a generalized infection with yeast. They have told their patients when asked, that the idea is nonsense and if that condition were present the person would probably be close to death. Indeed, generalized yeast infections spreading throughout the body do occur in people with advanced illness, such as cancer, and in people who have had their immune systems compromised by drugs, which suppress the immune system, or infections which destroy the effectiveness of the immune system. We are not talking about generalized yeast infection throughout the body.

What we are talking about is a sensitivity to the yeast which has colonized on the mucous membranes, such as vaginal or the gastrointestinal tract, extending from the mouth to the anus, or respiratory tract from nose to lungs. The yeast may also be on the skin or even the nails. Everybody is exposed to yeast, but not everybody develops problems from yeast. Newborns may be exposed at the time of birth. Common yeast problems of children and infants are diaper rash and ear infections, which usually are treated with antibiotics and sometimes the insertion of tubes.

Women are particularly prone to yeast because the vagina presents a warm, moist environment which promotes yeast growth. Yeast also proliferates when people consume high sugar diets, when broad spectrum antibiotics are used, and in females when the progesterone level is high during premenstrual time, pregnancy, and the use of birth control pills. Yeast is not limited to the reproductive tract. It may invade any other tissue, such as the respiratory or gastrointestinal system.

Men are not spared from this condition, but because the yeast in men is usually in the respiratory or gastrointestinal tract, it is not as easily identified as in women who have a visible, identifiable discharge from the vagina when the yeast is located there.

Yeast may infect any sex at any age. The manifestations of this condition have some common denominators whenever it is found. The body systems most affected by the yeast are the brain and the female endocrine system. Any of the functions of the brain may be disordered. A person with this problem may suffer from significant depression, difficulty in thinking, problem coping with life situations, difficulty in concentration and thinking, irritability and often lethargy. The symptoms vary from individual to individual and in the same individual from time to time.

There are further problems which can result if the yeast is in the gastrointestinal tract. The yeast may proliferate anywhere along the tract from the mouth to the anus. Yeast in the mouth, called thrush, results in soreness and white, cotton-like patches may be noticed. Further down in the esophagus yeast may cause difficulty or discomfort in swallowing. If the yeast is in the stomach and small intestine, bloating after eating and excessive gas are the general result. When invasion of the large intestine occurs, there is a characteristic problem with bowels, often an alternating diarrhea and constipation. Itching of the rectum can be an annoying, uncomfortable and embarrassing problem.

When the primary site of yeast is in the respiratory system, there may be recurrent sinus problems, chronic cough and/or asthma. A well known actress came to my office in great distress because she was about to do a musical and was terrified that a chronic cough would prevent her from doing the show. I suspected a yeast problem from her description of symptoms. She then told me that she had to leave town for a tour with the show in a few days. To her great fortune the first stop was Birmingham. A quick call to Dr. Truss, the appointment was set up on her arrival, and in two weeks, when the show opened, she was able to perform without any significant problems. Not everyone is as lucky in having such a quick response, but it does happen.

A most important consequence of the yeast sensitivity is the promotion of other sensitivities to foods and environmental factors such as weeds, grasses, animal dander and other inhalants. These sensitivities may cause problems with any system of the body resulting in such diverse symptoms as bone and joint aches, weight gain unresponsive to low calorie diets, headaches, skin problems, digestive and respiratory symptoms, depression, anxieties, fatigue with its subsequent psychological loss of self esteem and confidence.

The diagnosis of candidiasis depends on a careful history, and I have found the use of the laboratory helpful in confirming my suspicions. A history is what happens during your first visit to the doctor's office. Taking a history, questioning and listening, are among the most useful tools available to the physician. The doctor wants to know what your problems are, your complaints, your symptoms. Why did you seek help? What do you want changed, fixed up? Based on your complaints the doctor begins to formulate some ideas of what might be happening to cause those problems. By the time the first visit is finished, the physician should know what your most distressing symptoms are, how they affect you, how long they have been bothering you, and all you may know about them. Some people are able to give a very clear, concise history and don't require much questioning on the part of the doctor. Others need to be questioned in detail. The physician is also going to want details about your past experiences with illness and injuries, past treatments for the present illness and other illnesses, something about how and with whom you live, illnesses which your family may be prone to develop. At the end of the history taking, the physician should have a reasonable idea of how to proceed with any laboratory confirmations or treatments if laboratory is not needed.

In the early 1980s there was not a reliable laboratory test for candidiasis and treatment proceeded if the history was suggestive for this problem. In the mid eighties, Immunodiagnostic Laboratory of San Leandro, California (1-800 888-1113), under the direction of Ed Winger, M.D., one of the few Board Certified Immuno Pathologists, developed a test to indicate if the body has responded immunologically to yeast. The test does not diagnose yeast as a cause of symptoms, but it is helpful in separating the people who may have this problem from those who have not responded immunologically and may not have the problem.

The reason that it is desirable to separate those who might respond from treatment from those who have little chance in responding is that, when treatment is beneficial, it needs to be continued for a period of two to three years in most instances. Treatment is directed to reducing the yeast colonies to the lowest level possible. The theory is that the overgrowth of yeast has caused the immune system to be overwhelmed and give up the fight. By reducing the amount of yeast, the immune system

111

begins to function again and has a good chance of keeping further exposures under reasonable control. Whether the theory is correct or not is not known. What is known is that when there is an initial response to the therapy, treatment must be continued for a number of years in order to maintain improvement. I've seen many patients who, after several successful months on treatment, lacking the motivation of daily illness to keep them under a treatment program, become much less conscientious about their treatment and in short time return to my office complaining of the same symptoms which brought them in initially.

Treatment has taken different specific forms, depending on who is ordering it. Treatment of candidiasis is not a self help treatment. One should have the advantage of seeking help from someone who has had experience in the treatment and diagnosis of this condition. Since the symptoms of candidiasis resemble the symptoms of many other illnesses, a careful diagnosis must be made before treatment is started. Candidiasis does affect many more people than were suspected even a few years ago, but it is not the answer to all illnesses in mankind.

In general terms treatment is directed towards providing a hostile environment for the yeast, an environment which inhibits rather than promotes yeast growth. Treatment usually encompasses medication, supplements and dietary manipulation.

Dietary manipulation varies from practitioner to practitioner. Everyone does agree that the refined carbohydrates, sugars, enriched white flour, quick-cooking rice and the concentrated carbohydrates such as honey should be avoided. Yeast grows on sugars. That is why every recipe for yeast bread includes a small amount of concentrated carbohydrate in the form of sugar or honey. If one takes out the natural food for the yeast, growth is diminished. In this instance it is important to remember that natural fruits contain a considerable amount of sugar. I advise limiting fruit consumption to two fruits daily and try to limit to the low carbohydrate fruits, such as those allowable fruits listed in the hypoglycemic diet.

Further dietary manipulation eliminates yeast, mold and fungus foods. When a person has developed a sensitivity to the yeast in their system, they usually are sensitive to the yeast in foods. Although yeast and mold may be found in many foods, I have found the following limitations satisfactory in most instances. Yeast is found in bakery products, alcoholic drinks and vinegar. Aged, moldy cheeses should be eliminated. Mushrooms, a fungus food, are eliminated. Truffles are also fungi, but since truffles don't appear with any degree of regularity in the diet of most people I know or see in my office, the advice to avoid them is usually neglected. But if you should be a truffle user and have candidiasis, beware.

The medication and supplements are becoming more diverse. The anti yeast medication used most is Nystatin, a prescription drug which has been utilized for many years to fight yeast. It is one of the few prescription drugs with practically no listed side effects. There are more powerful antifungal medications available, but they carry the possibility of some potentially harmful side effects, and since this treatment is usually lengthy, I have avoided prescribing them. Other products containing caprylic acid have been described in the literature as antifungal. They have been reintroduced and have been utilized by some in the treatment of candidiasis. These drugs depend on the direct destructive action of the caprylic acid on the yeast cell and therefore have proven useful where the drug can come into contact with the yeast, such as the GI tract, vagina and skin.

Intestinal organisms which are normal in our system and are natural yeast fighters are usually prescribed. In the past several years many strains of acidophilus and other gastrointestinal organisms have been made available for supplementation. The normalization of these organisms in the gastrointestinal tract is an important part of the treatment. These organisms are de-

113

stroyed easily by broad spectrum antibiotics, such as tetracycline. The suggestion has been made that trace amounts of antibiotics found in our meat products have reduced the amount of these organisms significantly.

Other supplements said to exert anti yeast properties are garlic, which is available in odorless capsules, and a tea called *pau d' arco*. There have been some problems in relying on the potency of the *pau d' arco*, which is derived from the bark of a tree. Various companies have put out a brand of *pau d' arco*, not inexpensive, and varying in its potency. Because of the variation in potency, it is difficult to suggest its use without proper assurances from the companies preparing the product.

Many vitamins from the B family are derived from yeast. When supplements are taken by someone who has candidiasis, they must be careful to take only those vitamins which state clearly on the label that they are yeast free.

When treatment is started, Nystatin or the other natural yeast killers are started at a low level. It has been observed that as the yeast is killed by these substances, symptoms increase in intensity due to the substances released by the yeast to which the individual is sensitive. Starting slowly and working up to the maximum dosage within several days is preferable to a massive kill off of the yeast within a short period of time.

Response time varies, but it is not unusual to see clear evidence of positive response within the first few weeks of treatment, even when symptoms have been present for a long time. The key to successful treatment rests in part on the persistence of treatment over two to three years. Even with continuation of treatment the course is not always smooth. Some people have shown recurrent periods of symptoms during the time they have been treated. However, when treatment is successful, these recurrences generally get further apart, are less severe and have a shorter duration.

After a few months or longer of treatment, when symptoms

have been reduced, it may be advisable, if the response has been less than what was expected or acceptable, to search for the presence of food sensitivities, as candidiasis does lead to the promotion of food sensitivities. In some cases, when the candidiasis improves, the sensitivities to foods and inhalants diminish. In other cases, especially when the food sensitivities have been present for a long time, the sensitivities seem to have developed a life of their own and must be dealt with on their own.

Suggested reading:

The Missing Diagnosis, C. Orian Truss, M.D.

The Yeast Syndrome, John Park Trowbridge and Morton Walker

The Yeast Connection, William Crook, M.D.

CHAPTER 13

Food Sensitivities and Mood

ANOTHER CAUSE of mood disturbance, such as depression, may be food sensitivities. The sensitivities rarely result in just one pronounced symptom, such as depression, but are usually responsible for numerous complaints. Any system of the body may be affected by food sensitivities. For example, some symptoms may be headaches, fuzziness of thinking, lack of energy, breathing difficulties, abdominal pains, constipation, behavioral disorders, joint aches, fluid retention and these are but a few. Depression is usually part of the total picture, and part of that depression may be the result of a psychological reaction to the other symptoms ranging from annoying to disabling.

Two types of reactions occur when foods to which the individual is sensitive are eaten. The first is called an immediate reaction and is usually very easy to identify. When a person eats something and experiences some pronounced symptoms anywhere from several seconds up to an hour later, usually the offending food is quickly discovered and subsequently avoided. The immediate reaction rarely causes a diagnostic challenge.

The second type of reaction is a delayed reaction; the delay may be up to a few days. As you might imagine, considerable

116

difficulty would be encountered in trying to relate a feeling of malaise and headache occurring on Tuesday to a rice pudding eaten on Sunday. It is the delayed reaction which presents the most challenge in diagnosis.

Sometimes the controversy surrounding this subject, and controversy does exist, relates to semantics more than practical matters. Technically these reactions should not be called allergies, because the immune response in the body which occurs in allergies does not occur with the delayed food reactions. From a practical matter of "finding out what's wrong" and "What do I do to get better?" which is what my patients are interested in, it seems to matter very little if these reactions, which have the potential for causing so much human misery, are called allergy or sensitivity.

Uncovering the offending foods presents a formidable task. A variety of methods have been used, all with some success. Challenging with the suspected food, after eliminating it from the diet for about five days, is one method. Another method of challenging is with food extracts taken under the tongue and then observing the occurrence of symptoms. These two methods are time consuming, may be expensive and the results are frequently questionable.

The lack of reliability of the most common test, skin scratches, almost eliminates this type of testing for any serious investigation. The use of extracts injected under the skin and then observed for a reaction of swelling is more reliable, and more uncomfortable and takes a long time.

There are new blood tests measuring substances in the blood which are increased when delayed food sensitivities are present. These substances are called immunoglobulins (Ig). There are different immunoglobulins, but the ones of interest when trying to determine food sensitivities are of the G class. They are called immunoglobulin G (IgG). The immunoglobulin G has a number of components. Some are increased with the immediate

117

reaction, which is not so important because of the ease in identifying the immediate reaction; some are increased with the delayed reaction, which is the type of reaction we are most interested in uncovering. Advantages of the new blood testing are that it is reproducible and it determines the degree of sensitivity in the food tested.

At present these tests are available in some parts of the United States, but be aware of exactly which immunoglobulin is being tested. Our interest is primarily with the immunoglobulins of the G class, since these seem to be the ones effected in cases of delayed sensitivities. Blood for testing may be transported with special instructions. Those interested may contact or have their physician contact the following laboratories:

Quantum Analytical Laboratory
38 D Anna Cade Road
Rockwall, Texas 75087
(214) 771-4422

Immuno-Nutritional Clinical Laboratory
7404 Fulton Ave #5
North Hollywood, California 91605
(818) 503-5911
(800) 344-4646

Treatment of food sensitivities always depends on the elimination of the targeted food. The advantage of testing for a lot of foods is that finding out what you can eat, as well as what should be avoided, is of great importance. Most of the time, the delayed food sensitivities are to foods which are eaten three or more times per week. After avoidance of the food, anywhere from one to several months, depending on the degree of sensitivity, the food may be reintroduced. As long as that food is not eaten several times weekly, there is little chance of recurrence of the sensitivity.

This discussion of food sensitivities was introduced because

of its importance as a possible cause for significant mood disturbance. A suggested reading list follows for those interested in
further information.

Suggested reading:

Dr Mandell's 5-Day Allergy Relief System, Marshall Mandell,
M.D., Pocket Books, New York

Food, Mind & Mood, David Sheinkin, M.D., Michael
Schachter, M.D. and Richard Hutton, Warner Books

The Allergic Gourmet, June Roth, M.S., Empire Publications.
This is a good cookbook which my patients with sensitivities
have found very helpful. It may be ordered from Empire Publications, 1057 Oakland Ct., #101; Teaneck, NJ 07666; $15.95
including handling and shipping.

The Food Sensitivity Diet, Doug Kaufmann with Racquel Skol-
nik, Freundlich Books. Available in hardcover and paperback.

PART 4

Treatments for Depression

CHAPTER 14

Medication for Depression

"A STEAMING CUP of coffee, a frosty mug of beer, a couple of aspirin, a tranquilizer, a marijuana cigarette, and the innocent looking white powder that is heroin have one thing in common: they are drugs," writes Sheila Carroll in *Handbook for the Home,* the 1973 Yearbook of Agriculture.

"Amphetamines have been used to excess as pep pills and diet pills. Barbiturate sleeping pills are addicting and, in one sense, more dangerous than heroin since sudden withdrawal from heavy use of barbiturates can cause death. The combination of barbiturates and alcohol can have the same result.

"Perhaps half a million people are directly affected by these drugs. Mood-altering drugs have accounted for nearly a fourth of all the prescriptions issued by physicians in the course of a year."

Miss Carroll goes on to say that these figures reflect on our drug-taking habits as a nation. "There is reason to fear not only that drugs are taken too freely and prescribed too easily, but also that their very abundance is creating a climate in which drug abuse cannot help but flourish. Americans of all ages are using drugs in greater numbers than ever before. Virtually every

TREATMENTS FOR DEPRESSION

category of pharmacologic agent that has some sort of effect on mood is being misused at this time.''

Writing in *Dr. Atkins' Diet Revolution,* Dr. Robert C. Atkins said that, in these take-a-pill-for-whatever-ails-you times, it is hardly a surprise that some of our drugs designed to "help" people have side effects that do just the opposite.

"A good example: the more potent psycho drugs." The major categories of such potent medicines are the phenothiazines (such as Thorazine and Compazine) and the psychic energizer groups (Elavil and Sinequan, for example). My own clinical observations, as yet unproven, suggest that both seem to increase insulin output and lead to weight gain and hypoglycemia (low blood sugar). This may not be true of the milder drugs such as Librium, Valium, meprobamate.

"Because hypoglycemia is so often the root cause of psychoneurotic symptoms such as depression and anxiety, it is hypoglycemics who are very likely to receive these drugs. You can see how such drugs, useful as they are, can, if your problem is really hypoglycemia, provide more harm than benefit.''

Dr. Atkins reported that in working with hundreds of psychiatric patients, he has found the high-protein, low-carbohydrate diet has sometimes been more effective than the drugs in stabilizing the mental symptoms the patients were experiencing. "In many cases, working with the patient's psychiatrist, we were able to reduce the dosage of these potent drugs, and, in some cases, discontinue them completely, as patients began to show a sometimes miraculous and dramatic improvement in their depression, anxiety, and adjustment problems.''

Richard J. Turchetti and Joseph J. Morella, writing in *New Age Nutrition,* state that users of drugs become so dependent that a heavy dose can cause a temporary toxic psychosis (mental derangement), usually accompanied by hallucinations. Prolonged or habitual users sometimes develop suicidal tendencies and risk accidental death from barbiturate poisoning.

124

MEDICATION FOR DEPRESSION

"Barbiturates are physically addictive." Turchetti and Morella continue. "Tolerance develops and withdrawal symptoms occur when the user stops taking the drug. There are many withdrawal symptoms, including restlessness, abdominal cramps, nausea and vomiting, weakness, shaking, delirium, insomnia, delusions and convulsions. It is dangerous to allow this withdrawal process to continue without proper medical treatment."

The minor tranquilizers (Miltown, Equanil, Librium, Valium, etc.) are similar to the barbiturates-hypnotics in most actions, but they tend to be more relaxing of skeletal muscles, more selective in the relief of anxiety, less hypnotic, and less liable to produce uncoordination of movement or to impair judgment, Turchetti and Morella point out. They are also less likely to produce coma, respiratory failure, and death from overdosage (except for meprobamate), and are a little less liable to produce psychological dependence.

The two authors quote *Lancet*, the British medical journal, for February 4, 1961, as saying that the mildest of the three principal types of tranquilizers are those made from meprobamate (Miltown, Equanil, etc.) But continued or excessive use of these has been associated with drowsiness, failure of muscular coordination, coma, low blood pressure, convulsions and weakness. According to Richard J. Turchetti and Joseph J. Morella, the most potent of the tranquilizers are the chlordiazepoxide compounds (e.g., Librium). They are said to depress so greatly as to reproduce a choking action.

"Tranquilizers can treat only symptoms; they rarely cure anything," Turchetti and Morella say. "Furthermore they tend to mask symptoms that the doctor could find helpful in diagnosing the patient's problem. Moreover, Dr. Otis R. Farley, director of the Medical and Surgical Branch of St. Elizabeth's Hospital, Washington, D. C., has discovered, for example, that many popular drugs can alter the body's ability to fight infections.

125

Others can cause skin rash and affect the function of the adrenal glands and the entire enzyme system.''

One way that drugs may inhibit the body's ability to deal with infections is to deplete the vitamin reserves. ''Drugs are generally foreign, alien substances, not normally found in the body,'' remind Dr. Harold Rosenberg and Dr. A. N. Feldzamen in *The Doctor's Book of Vitamin Therapy*. ''As a result, most drugs—even ordinary household non-prescription drugs, patent medicines and over-the-counter drugs—have a surprising toxicity, far above that of vitamins.''

Drs. Rosenberg and Feldzamen say that drugs are generally rapid in their action, while vitamins may be slow to take effect. ''Many drugs have only a narrow and specific effectiveness, while vitamins are often systemic in their action, tending to influence the whole body. One single vitamin may affect many tissues and functionings—skin, hair, mouth conditions, muscle spasms, cardiac stress, ulcers, mental state, vitality, etc.''

They add that drugs are usually most effective when they are given alone, so that other powerful biochemical agents cannot interfere with their functioning, while vitamins seem to work best in combinations, especially those combinations (with minerals) that in total provide good or optimal nutrition. I would only add that these combinations probably work best because that is how vitamins and minerals appear in nature; in foods, to be more specific.

''Anticonvulsants, the Pill and also another pharmacologically unrelated drug, the sedative glutethimide (Doriden), have been found capable of producing multiple vitamin deficiencies,'' states Dr. Daphne A. Roe in the October-November, 1973 issue of *Food and Nutrition News*. Her article is titled ''Nutritional Side Effects of Drugs.''

''The major incidence of drug induced deficiency states is in people on long term and multiple drug regimens,'' Dr. Roe continues. ''When a particular drug or drug group is necessary for the continued control of a disease, nutrient depletion takes place over time and it is impossible to stop drug intake to facilitate nutritional rehabilitation. In this situation, vitamin supplements, rather than massive doses of the missing nutrient, are required with maintenance of drug intake. Drug associated nutritional deficiencies are usually multifactorial. The drug increases requirements for a nutrient, the diet is insufficient for the needs of the individual, previous or present disease, such as chronic infection or alcoholism, also may interfere with nutritional status.''

The late Adelle Davis is another nutritionist who believed that drugs deplete vitamin stores. Writing in *Let's Get Well,* she said that all drugs, "by their toxicity, induce a condition of stress, which particularly increases the need for vitamin C, pantothenic acid, the antistress factors, and perhaps for every body requirement. Because most drugs can damage the liver, the body's demands for protein and vitamin E are also especially high. The more adequate the diet can be made, therefore, the more effective the drug, and the shorter the time it need be taken.''

In another book, *Let's Eat Right to Keep Fit,* Adelle Davis said: "It is difficult to realize what large amounts of vitamin C can be destroyed by drugs. It has long been known that if more of the vitamin is taken than is needed, the excess is quickly lost in the urine; and that none is lost until the tissues throughout the body are saturated, or contain all the vitamin C they need. A healthy person's tissues may be saturated with as little as 200 milligrams or less of the vitamin daily. Yet I found one study of the quantity of this vitamin needed by a number of persons taking tranquilizers; no vitamin C whatsoever appeared in the urine of several until 15 grams—15,000 milligrams—were given daily.

"In planning diets," she continues, "I usually suggest that 500 milligrams of vitamin C be taken with each dose of medica-

127

tion, and that if bruises appear, this amount be increased until the physician decreases the drug. It is known, however, that vitamin C increases the value of every type of drug and at the same time decreases its toxicity.''

Another danger in prescribing some drugs is mentioned by Harald J. Taub in *Keeping Healthy in a Polluted World*. He discusses a report by Dr. Thorne Butler, who analyzed blood samples of drivers suspected by the Las Vegas, Nevada police of driving under the influence of alcohol. Dr. Butler says that 20 per cent of those who are picked up for erratic driving have little or no alcohol in their blood; their supposed drunkenness is the result of sedatives and tranquilizers that their doctors have prescribed for their nerves.

"Even among the 80 per cent who do have appreciable levels of blood alcohol, 16 per cent are also sedated by drugs," Taub says. "So be aware that those pills that improve your ability to cope with pressure at the office may be precisely what will render you unable to cope with the emergencies of driving.''

A more alarming situation is that of overmedication of children. About three-quarters of the thousands of drugs that are available for adults are not approved for the treatment of children, according to the Food and Drug Administration.

"Admittedly, it is difficult to obtain valid test data regarding drug effects in children," states Richard C. Thompson in *FDA Consumer*, March, 1975. "There have been no real guidelines, despite the enlightened research atmosphere of the past two decades. Results obtained from tests in adults cannot be transferred necessarily to children.

"Also, children are growing and maturing; their brains and body systems are not sufficiently stabilized to permit absolute decisions as to medical treatment and accurate prediction of results. Yet children do become ill and injured; they do require care and treatment and hospitalization. What can the physician do when three of every four drugs available are not for use in children?''

Under the circumstances, most physicians ignore the disclaimer on the label of the drug and, based on their knowledge and experience, use an adult drug in what they presume to be a child's dose. Although a drug may not have been specifically approved for pediatric use, the judgment and experience of the physician is a factor in so many medical decisions that it is difficult to quarrel with it in such a case. The medical profession has not been satisfied with this situation, however, and has claimed that the problem of pediatric drugs deserves more precise resolution.

According to *FDA Consumer,* the American Academy of Pediatrics emphasizes the need to balance the risk involved in the use of a particular new drug against the benefit the child patient is expected to receive. It repeatedly stresses that the benefit must be substantial if the risk is known to exist, whether the patient is an infant suffering from meningitis or an adolescent being treated for depression.

Tranquilizers also pose a threat to unborn children, according to a report in the December 12, 1974 issue of *The New York Times.* Two tranquilizers, meprobamate and chlordiazepoxide (Miltown, Equanil and Librium) may cause serious birth defects if taken during the first six weeks of pregnancy, the newspaper states. The study in question examined 19,044 live births and concluded that nonbarbiturate tranquilizers may be harmful to the fetus.

''By placing controls on Valium and Librium—two of the Nation's leading prescription drugs—the Federal Government has hoisted a warning flag. It is saying, in effect, that when used correctly, these drugs are safe, but that they have demonstrated potential for abuse,'' writes Margaret Morrison in the April, 1975 issue of *FDA Consumer.* Her article is titled '' 'Cooling It' on Tranquilizers.''

129

TREATMENTS FOR DEPRESSION

The FDA recommended that Valium and Librium be placed under control, because continued consumption of high doses of these drugs can lead to dependence on them, the agency told the Justice Department's Drug Enforcement Agency. A prescription for either drug is valid for only six months and can be refilled only five times. The new regulations also require recordkeeping by pharmacists, distributors and manufacturers and set criminal penalties for illegal use. The regulations do not put limits on the number of pills that can be prescribed in one prescription.

After high usage, abstinence can then produce withdrawal symptoms that include delirium, trembling, psychosis and exaggeration of reflexes, the article continues. If untreated these symptoms can be fatal, although such cases are extremely rare, the FDA said.

The controls also apply to several related drugs of the benzodiazepine class—Dalmane, Serax, Tranxene.

"It is not known just how much effect the new controls will have in curbing the widespread use of the drugs," the article reports. "In the past two years, a stricter control of amphetamines—no refills and only written prescriptions—cut use of these drugs by an estimated 50 to 60 per cent.

"Regardless of whether the new controls cut down substantially on the use of Valium and Librium, they should point up to consumers and physicians that these two drugs should not be taken routinely or carelessly. They should be used with restraint."

By citing the disadvantages, I do not mean to imply that medication should never be used. When used properly under correct supervision, drugs can be effective and an important part of the treatment program. In some cases medication is the best treatment. Sometimes, however, patients will object to taking medication.

"I've been through so much, doctor, but I don't want a

crutch,'' Catherine told me on her first visit. She is a woman in her seventies who, until a few years ago, was active in business. Gradually she became obsessed with how ill she was and it became difficult for her to concentrate on business affairs. She even found it difficult to communicate with others because she was preoccupied with her illness.

She eventually became more sad, more hopeless, and, when her ability to concentrate diminished and her depression became more acute, she left work for good. After a few attempts to seek help, she was referred to me. At first she refused medication, so we proceeded without the usual tranquilizers and anti-depressants. I think the wishes of the patient must be respected if those wishes are within reason. Certainly starting treatment without medication in respect to her wish was reasonable. However, as time went by, she became more depressed, and I insisted that if I were to continue as her physician we would have to do it my way. She agreed to the medication and began to show enough signs of improvement that she started volunteer work.

But the medication ''bugged'' her and, not wanting a crutch as she put it, she drifted away from the once-a-month office visit and at the same time drifted away from regular medication. After about three months, she called, sounding almost as desperate as she did during her initial visit. This time, realizing the magnitude of her problem, she requested medication immediately.

Of course, drugs were not the only treatment that I used on Catherine. Her environment was changed by putting her in the hospital, and another physician, who specialized in internal medicine, examined her and attended to some of her physical complaints. She was given a special high-protein diet, low in sugar, and many vitamins. She was also seen in a supportive type of psychotherapy. The end result was that a combination of these methods contributed to her getting well. In her case, though, the medications were a necessary stepping stone so that she would be receptive to our other treatments.

Before a physician prescribes medication, he has to consider many variables. He must determine the type of depression; the extent to which the patient is agitated and withdrawn; the physical state of the patient; how he has responded to medications in the past; is the patient able to follow instructions or is he willing to cooperate with someone who will administer the medication; the suicidal risk of the patient.

The analysis of this data will more than likely determine the medication to be administered. The major tranquilizers are generally suggested for schizophrenic disorders. The minor tranquilizers, such as Librium and Valium, are so widely prescribed for any emotional upset that they have become a household word. It would be unusual to be with a group of people and find that none of them was carrying one of the minor tranquilizers "just in case."

The other group of drugs prescribed for depressions are known appropriately as anti-depressants. A study at the Veterans Administration Hospital in Palo Alto, California, conducted by Dr. Leo Hollister and his associates, indicated that the major tranquilizers were especially effective in the depressions that are characterized by great agitation. The depressions characterized by a withdrawal of the patient responded better to one of the anti-depressants. (L. E. Hollister, J. E. Overall, J. Shelton, V. Pennington, I. Kimbell and M. Johnson, "Drug Therapy of Depression—Amitriptyline, Perphenazine, and Their Combination in Different Syndromes," *Archives of General Psychiatry,* 17: 486–493, 1967).

The point that I am making is that there are many types of tranquilizers and antidepressants, and it is up to the physician to recommend the medication that is most suitable for the condition. Generally the medication is used concurrently with some type of psychotherapy.

MEDICATION FOR DEPRESSION

Every few years the medical profession and the public is barraged with information about the newest psychiatric miracle drug which promises greater effectiveness, quicker action and fewer side effects than the medications on the market at that time. BUYER, BE AWARE. The claims usually become modified at a later date, following increased usage which results in the new drug being more common than miraculous.

The patient should know that it may take several days to several weeks before an antidepressant is effective. The exceptions are the amphetamines, which change a person's mood in a matter of minutes. These are rarely prescribed because their effectiveness is temporary, leaving the patient with a big letdown. A more alarming disadvantage is the fact that, as one builds up a tolerance for the drug, more and more of the medication is needed to give results. One man who saw me in consultation was buying amphetamines by the pound because he had taken the drug for years and needed more and more as time went by. In my opinion, this drug is usually not the right one for depression.

Unfortunately, drugs, as we know, have many side effects. The most annoying is dryness of mouth. Sometimes there is excessive perspiration, blurring of vision, excitement, menstrual disturbances, rapid heartbeat, to name a few. In general, these side effects are not fatal, even though some, like mouth dryness, are very uncomfortable. But, of course, a physician will only prescribe these drugs in extreme cases. If the patient were to choose between the side effects and the depression, he would usually choose the side effects. Where megavitamin therapy is administered, eventually the drugs hopefully can be discarded. Smaller doses of the major tranquilizers can be used in schizophrenia when the patient is on large vitamin doses.

There are some antidepressants that may cause serious side effects. These drugs belong to a group known as monoamine oxidase inhibitors (MAO inhibitors). The name was chosen be-

133

cause it describes where these drugs work in the body, namely, to inhibit the chemical monoamine oxidase. The monoamine oxidase is necessary to break down another chemical, a neurotransmitter, which is responsible for transmitting the nervous impulse from one nerve cell to another.

By giving the MAO inhibitor, this neurotransmitter is built up in greater concentrations since it is not destroyed as quickly. This class of antidepressants is sometimes prescribed by the physician, because at times they will work where everything else has failed. When drugs from this class are used, special precautions must be given to the patient, since they are not compatible with some medications, alcohol, and certain foods such as cheddar cheese, herring and liver.

Used properly and under the direction of competent physicians, the danger is minimal. Some drugs in this class are available, and they may be prescribed for very obstinate cases of depression.

One of the interesting aspects of these medications is that they have stimulated research into the biochemical nature of depression. I wish that I could say that depression is the result of a biochemical malfunction, increasing the need for vitamins and minerals, but the situation is more complex. This may be the case but oftentimes it is not. Other measures are often required to bring results. Research into the method of action of the antidepressants leads to the neurotransmitters, but the final answer has not yet been found.

In general, both classes of antidepressants influence a change in the chemicals known as neurotransmitters, although there is conflicting evidence concerning the role of neurotransmitters in depression. Also the inevitable "which came first, the chicken or the egg?" aspects have not yet been answered to everyone's satisfaction. In other words, does the mood change the biochemistry, or does the biochemistry change the mood? There are four possibilities: 1) the mood changes the biochemistry; 2) the biochemistry changes the mood; 3) both 1 and 2 are correct; 4) the question of chemistry is irrelevant and other explanations for depression must be sought.

The person who is experiencing depression need not be concerned about the controversy, only secure in the fact that there are medications available which will work for him. These medications might be regarded as a crutch by some, but no more so than the need for penicillin to treat the more stubborn cases of pneumonia. In the hands of a competent physician, I have full confidence in the antidepressants for some forms of depression. Ideally, however, we all hope that the patient progresses to such a stage that these medications are not necessary.

CHAPTER 15

Lithium

NOT ALL PILLS prescribed to treat depression are synthesized in the laboratory. Some therapies utilize substances found in nature. Lithium is one of those natural materials. In my opinion, the use of lithium—a silvery white trace mineral found in rocks, mineral water, natural brines, etc.—is one of the most significant developments in the field of psychiatry in the last 20 years. It is one of the few agents that can be monitored easily by means of periodic tests to determine if the dosage is proper. When given to a patient who is able to understand the need for caution and the use of periodic blood testing, and when administered by a competent physician, it is a safe, effective and relatively inexpensive treatment that has already restored a full life to thousands of happy and grateful people.

"Studies show that 80 per cent of manic-depressives undergoing a manic phase are quieted within five to 14 days on [lithium]," report Rona Cherry and Laurence Cherry in the November 25, 1973 issue of *The New York Times Magazine*. "Continuing the patients on the mineral blocks further manic highs and also many lows; it also has been found helpful in preventing, or at least easing, further depressions for persons who have already experienced simple 'unipolar' depressions."

LITHIUM

In modern times, lithium was first used in psychiatric conditions by an Australian psychiatrist John F. J. Cade. He describes its use in "Lithium Salts in the Treatment of Psychotic Excitement," (*Medical Journal of Australia*, 36:349-352, 1949). Because of Dr. Cade's initial work, studies were undertaken in the early 1950s by Dr. Mogens Schou and his colleagues in Denmark (M. Schou, N. Juel-Nielsen, E. Strongren and H. Voldby, "The Treatment of Manic Psychosis by the Administration of Lithium Salts," *J. Neurol. any UROS. Psychiatry*, 17:250-260, 1954), and later by Dr. Samuel Gershon, whose work at the University of Melbourne, Australia, encouraged physicians at the University of Michigan to try lithium in 1960. That trial in 1960 ended almost a decade of ignoring the possible use of lithium in psychiatric disorders.

Other researchers followed up with systematic studies in universities and clinics. Dr. Ronald Fieve at The New York State Psychiatric Institute is a prominent investigator of lithium. Many others have conducted lithium trials and now an impressive collection of data is available which confirms the original supposition of Dr. Cade that lithium is an effective agent in the treatment of disorders of the mood ("Lithium in the Treatment of Mood Disorders," Public Health Service Publication No. 2143, 1970).

When I first saw Elaine as a patient, I was close to finishing my psychiatric training and very much influenced by, but not completely accepting, the popular premise that uncovering the hidden traumas, the conflicts, repressed fears, the disordered sexuality was the proper path for a psychiatrist to pursue in helping the patient. But such was my training and psychotherapy was the tool most familiar to me. So Elaine, a single, middle-aged executive secretary, and I were off on the psychotherapeutic trail.

We met twice a week, 45 minutes each time, and, over the years, a definite pattern of mood disturbance was observed.

137

TREATMENTS FOR DEPRESSION

About four times a year with certain regularity she developed a moderate depression, which would be a little less severe after about four to six weeks. Gradually her mood would change, she would become less and less depressed; finally, she would be slightly elated (hypomanic), which she described as "zippy."

One could assess her mood at a glance. When she was depressed her face lacked color; eyes were dull; her grooming was neglected, although, because of her work, she was always neat. Her face appeared sad and occasionally she was tearful. Her speech was slower than usual and her voice was quiet. Altogether she presented the pitiful appearance of a little woman, all alone, almost but not quite beaten by life; almost but not quite ready to give up. When she was elated she was a different person. There was a joy that emanated from her that made you forget her age. She was vivacious with a sense of humor that was infectious. Unfortunately for her and her friends, these periods of euphoria only lasted for a few days. Inevitably she would sink into one of her down moods.

After years of working together, I discussed an observation that I had made. Her depressions often followed a run-in with a friend. The difficulty could be anything from a disagreement, which she interpreted as an insult, to a rejection, real or imagined, on the part of a friend. At one time she became depressed when two of her close friends went away for a weekend without asking her to join them. Another time she was upset for weeks when a new friend was not thoughtful enough to drive her home but allowed her to use public transportation. These losses and rejections were tied up into a neat psychological package relating to rejection as a child. For a while I was very proud of my deductions, but my pride was shattered in the following months when, in spite of the revelations, her pattern of depression every three months continued.

Since I had prescribed the available antidepressants, there were not many choices left to try. About this time lithium was

138

becoming available for use and study in manic-depressive illnesses. I discussed it with her and she readily accepted the idea
of using anything that might help overcome the awful mood
changes that she was experiencing. For the first few months on
lithium, she had a change of pattern that was puzzling for her
and certainly unwelcome. Instead of having depressions every
three months, she began to experience definite depressive symptoms every two weeks. This lasted two or three days. As the
year passed, the depressions became farther and farther apart
and less severe. Eventually she was experiencing what she described as one or two bad days every six months. The bad days
were nowhere near the depressive symptoms which she used to
have, but there were days in which she was aware that her
energy was a little down and her mood was slightly depressed.
During these down days she was able to continue work as
she had always done, but her social life—which used to be
interrupted frequently—continued almost as if nothing had hap-
pened. These days were more of a slight feeling of sadness
rather than being depressed. She knew that the feeling would
pass quickly. As for the "zippy" feelings she used to experience, she described her present sensation as: "I feel like I
would become zippy but something is keeping a clamp on me."
These feelings were also experienced for a short time, but
only a few times a year. Office visits were spaced out from
two times a week in the beginning to two times a year after
she had been on lithium for about a year and a half. I had
always felt that psychotherapy gave her the support she needed
through the difficult times, when all she could do was get herself to work. But the lithium did more than support her; it
changed her pattern and made her better.
The story of Elaine is not an unusual one. Thousands of
people around the world, who are subjected to repeated mood
disturbances, have, with lithium, once again been able to live
12 months out of every year, instead of experiencing the waste

of time on a regular basis because of psychiatric illness. Another advantage is the elimination of time and money spent in a treatment such as psychotherapy that was only moderately successful. In the case of Elaine, psychotherapy did offer support. Without it and the psychotherapeutic relationship there were many times when I thought she would have given up completely. But in spite of what I thought I was doing in psychotherapy, I was only treating the effect of the disease and making it a little more tolerable. Psychotherapy was not treating the cause. After lithium was administered for many months, psychotherapy was eliminated.

The use of lithium described so far is for the condition known as manic-depressive. Manic state is characterized by unending energy, sense of elation, hyperactivity, unbounded optimism and, in general, the opposite clinical picture of depression. Just as the depressed person sees gloom everywhere, the manic person sees hope and promise.

A patient of mine who is subject to both disorders of mood (elation and depression) was first seen in a manic state. During this time she was buying a good deal of trivia and making plans to expand her business. Money was no object and she required very little sleep. She was expansive in her mood and in relationships with whomever she came into contact. Within a month the manic episode started to fade and a mild depression took over. She was aghast at the money she had spent and was alarmed that she might not be able to regain her losses. In reality there was very little change in her life situation or in her finances, but there was a great change in her attitude toward them.

Since the manic and depressive states are often related, it was natural that lithium would be tried as a treatment for depression. Some of the earlier trials using lithium showed no improvement in those being treated for depression and in a few instances the depression became worse. And, as I have mentioned, the use of lithium was abandoned for a time.

The picture was further clouded in 1949, when the Food and Drug Administration banned the use of lithium chloride as a salt substitute. Lithium can apparently upset the sodium-potassium balance in the body, which can lead to kidney and circulation disorders. A few deaths have resulted from this sodium-potassium imbalance in patients who were unable to eliminate salt.

In 1963, a British psychiatrist, Dr. G. P. Hartigan, suggested that some individuals were protected from recurrent episodes of depression when lithium was administered. ("The Uses of Lithium Salts in Affective Disorders," *British Journal of Psychiatry*, 109:810-814, 1963). A controlled study of lithium's effect in depression was done at the National Institutes of Mental Health Clinical Center in Bethesda, Maryland by Drs. Goodwin, Murphy and Bunney (F. K. Goodwin, D. L. Murphy and W. E. Bunney, Jr., "Lithium in Depression and Mania: a Double-Blind Behavioral and Chemical Study," *Archives of General Psychiatry*, 21:486-496, 1969). In this study of 19 patients, two-thirds showed some improvement in their depression when treated with lithium.

The patients who responded were then given a pill that looked like lithium but was in fact a placebo containing mostly sugar or starch. Neither the physician nor the patient knew when the substitution was made. This method is called double-blind; that is, the subject first gets the pill being tested and then he gets a "nothing" pill to see if the results are different. The effect of substituting the sugar pill was that two-thirds of the patients that had shown some improvement with lithium became worse with the placebo. By subjecting these results to statistical analysis, the conclusion is drawn that there is a strong possibility that the improvement seen in the patients was due to the administration of lithium.

At present the studies which have been done indicate that

141

lithium is effective as a treatment for some cases of depression. It is also effective in some cases of recurrent depression to prevent or modify the recurrence so that the depression is not as severe as it usually is. From a practical standpoint in the treatment of depressive illness, I have found the most effective use of lithium is in those cases of recurrent depression, especially where there is no clear-cut cause for the depression— such as the ending of a personal relationship, loss of a job, medical illness, etc.

The use of lithium does not guarantee an absence of depression, but in a high percentage of the cases the depression is modified. I find that, in a person who may develop some depression while on lithium, the use of a regular antidepressant is helpful. As I mentioned, it may take several months on lithium before the full effect can be determined. In the case of Elaine, her pattern of depression changed over the first year.

Even though lithium is a naturally occurring element of nature, when it is taken in doses necessary for treatment of a psychiatric disorder, it must be done under the proper supervision. This mineral is not available in over-the-counter preparations. Administration of lithium must be done by trained professionals.

At high levels in the blood, lithium becomes a dangerous poison. That's why the blood of patients on lithium must be monitored. The early reluctance to use lithium, as I mentioned earlier, was related to some deaths that occurred when lithium was sold as a salt substitute for people who were on a low-salt diet because they were unable to eliminate salt from their systems. At the time little was known about lithium except that it tasted like salt. These deaths resulted because they were unable to eliminate the lithium that built up in their systems just as they were unable to eliminate salt.

It is important for the physician to establish, through routine physical and laboratory examination, that the patient's body is

LITHIUM

functioning well and eliminates salt properly. If a problem is established in the elimination of salts, it does not mean that lithium cannot be used, but it does mean that extra precautions—such as more frequent lithium testing in the blood—must be taken.

Side effects can be classified into early and late. The early side effects are usually due to rapid change in the blood level of lithium. They are not dangerous but they are certainly distressing. For the most part, the early effects may be avoided by gradually increasing the dosage of lithium, rather than starting on a full dose immediately. Early common side effects may be nausea, vomiting, diarrhea, abdominal pain, frequent urination and thirst, weakness and hand tremor.

Late side effects may include hand tremors, persistence of thirst and frequency of urination, small weight gain and possibly enlargement of the thyroid. These early and late side effects are to be distinguished from the more serious conditions of poisoning which occurs when the lithium level gets too high. Symptoms of poisoning can be divided into those affecting several body systems such as gastrointestinal, neuro-muscular, central nervous system and cardiovascular. In general there may be several symptoms such as nausea, vomiting, pulse irregularity and confusion, but there is usually a profound lethargy that develops before death.

The toxic manifestations appear gradually. The early symptoms of intoxication do bear a similarity to side effects mentioned both early and late. The distinguishing factor is that in intoxication the lithium level is high. If a person has been managed for a while on a satisfactory level of lithium, then develops side effects, it may be the beginning of lithium intoxication. The first thing that must be done is to have the blood tested for lithium to see if it is high. If the level is too high, all that is needed is a reduction of the lithium dosage. By reducing the dosage and watching the level closely, any serious effects of the poisoning are avoided.

Scientists have yet to unravel the mystery of just how lithium works in treating depression. Since lithium is a trace mineral, the reason may have biochemical or nutritional overtones. We don't know. We do know that some cases of depression are due to nutritional deficiencies. A deficiency in niacin (vitamin B3) brings on pellagra and dementia. A deficiency in pyridoxine (vitamin B6) can cause some women taking the Pill to become depressed. Depression can be caused by a deficiency in pantothenic acid, a B vitamin. When a patient has beriberi, a thiamine (vitamin B1) deficiency, depression is one of the symptoms. And so it goes. Therefore, the physician-psychiatrist must be aware of his patient's nutritional state, along with the mental, emotional and environmental state. The reason for depression is not always cut and dried.

CHAPTER 16

Amino Acid Therapy for Depression

AMINO ACIDS, NATURAL CHEMICALS which are the building blocks of proteins, were showing great promise in the treatment of depression when L-tryptophan, one of the most basic of the amino acids in this treatment program, was taken off the market because of some serious side effects, including some deaths.

Even though L-tryptophan had been sold over the counter for a number of years with no problems, the sudden emergence of the life threatening side effect made it necessary to halt all sales of L-trytophan.

Through careful studies all the serious problems caused by the L-tryptophan were traced back to one laboratory which changed its production method resulting in a sometimes fatal reaction. The Food and Drug Administration acted rapidly and correctly in removing L-tryptophan as soon as it was recognized that the side effects were connected with ingestion of the amino acid.

Don Tyson, President of Tyson Associates, Hawthorne, California, a premier distributor of amino acid products, has worked closely with those who studied and discovered the source of the problem. Even though there is very little mystery remaining

145

about the unfortunate manufacturing error, L-tryptophan, which had been used safely for years for depression, insomnia and pain control, has not been released for general consumption. Mr. Tyson has reported that there is a desire by the FDA to classify all amino acids as medication.

Priscilla Slagel, M.D. author of *The Way Up from Down,* published by Random House in 1987, reports that in most cases she is still having positive results in the treatment of depression with amino acids without using L-tryptophan. The use of amino acids as a therapy in depression and other medical illnesses is just beginning to be recognized and offers great promise for the future treatment of diseases.

Amino acids when joined together form proteins. Besides being the stuff from which muscles are made, proteins are the material which forms a whole group of substances called neurotransmitters. To understand the importance of neurotransmitters, it is helpful to have some knowledge of what the neurotransmitters are and how they work.

Nerve cells are responsible for controlling many functions of the body, not only the movements of our muscles, but also our thinking and mood. There are many kinds of nerve cells and although the function of one group of nerve cells may differ from another group, the general structure of all nerves is the same. In addition the way in which one nerve cell communicates with its neighboring nerve cell to get the message passed along is basically the same.

It is peculiar, but nerve cells don't touch one another. They come close, they have lots of little projections which come close to lots of projections on the next nerve cell, but they don't touch. It's as if the fingers of each of your hands were extended towards each other, coming very close, but never touching. And yet what happens in one nerve cell must be conveyed to the next nerve cell and on down the line for the impulse to get from where it started to where it's going. For example, if your brain is aware through its sense of sight and sound that an oncoming vehicle is in the same path you are occupying, not only must the information be processed through the thinking part of the brain to recognize the danger present, but also impulses must be sent through the nervous trails in the body to move your body very quickly. All these various types of neural activity take place through impulses being sent throughout the nervous system from one cell to the other.

The basic mechanism of transmission involves the storage of a chemical at one end of the nerve cell which, as the impulse is passed down the cell, causes a release of that chemical into the space between it and the adjacent nerve cell. The next cell must then absorb that chemical, which results in the impulse passing down the second cell. The impulse reaches the end of the second cell, causing the same type of neurotransmitter which is stored there to be released into the space between the second and third cell and so on down the line of nerve cells. It is important to note that the chemicals do not move down an entire cell. Once picked up by a cell they stay in exactly the same position until the work is done, at which time they are released back into the space from where they came. They are then reabsorbed from that space by the first cell, from where they were originally, and wait to start the whole process over again when another impulse is sent down the cell where they reside.

So we see each nerve cell has different mechanisms at each end of the cell. One side releases a chemical and then picks it up again. The other side picks up the chemical first, then releases it when it has done its work. The neurotransmitter passes through the stages of being released, picked up by a second cell, released and reabsorbed into the first cell from where it came.

There are many neurotransmitters in the body and they each seem to have some specific function related to the workings of the body. Even though they have different functions, the way in which they are stored and work to transmit the nervous impulse from one cell to the other seems to be the same as described above.

In order to transmit the impulse correctly, the neurotransmitter must be present in sufficient quantity to instruct the second cell to send the impulse along. The impulse only gets started when there is sufficient amount of the neurotransmitter present. When there is not enough of the neurotransmitter available, the nervous impulse is not started efficiently and all kinds of problems result, depending on which nerves and neurotransmitters are involved. If the neurotransmitters involved with mood are involved, then there may be a significant depression.

Let's get an idea of a few things that may go wrong along the pathway described during the progression of an impulse from one nerve to the next. First there may not be enough of the neurotransmitter stored at the end of the first cell. It may not be released properly. There may be a problem in accumulating the neurotransmitter in the space between the cells. The second cell may not be able to pick up enough of the neurotransmitter to get the message to start the impulse. The second cell may not release the chemical when it is finished with it. The first cell may not be able to pick up the neurotransmitter once it has been released by the second cell. And these are just a few of the problems which could be involved. With all the things which might go wrong, it sometimes becomes incomprehensible how anything could go right.

As we have seen, the common denominator seems to be not enough of the neurotransmitter, whatever the cause. Amino acid therapy attempts to correct that problem by overloading the system with the amino acids which form, or are the precursors to that particular neurotransmitter. By taking certain amino acids, natural substances, in unusually high doses, an attempt is made to force the body to form more of the neurotransmitter

148

desired and, in so doing, correct the abnormality, such as depression.

This therapy has been helpful, at times, when all other therapies have failed. It is of great interest that antidepressant medication is thought to be effective, for the very same reasons precursor therapy is thought to be effective, namely, it increases the concentration of desirable neurotransmitters.

The advantage claimed by use of the amino acid is the absence of side effects which accompany most antidepressant medications when taken at a therapeutic level. A word of caution, however: antidepressants that have been used for over 25 years have a history behind them. Perhaps not all side effects from the antidepressants are known, but after 25 years the probability is that most of the side effects have been described and are well documented, so any physician who prescribes the antidepressants has at his command the knowledge of possible side effects and possible dangers. There is not the same amount of background available on the use of individual amino acids at high levels. Much more experience has to be obtained before there is a complete understanding of all of the possible implications of consuming amino acids in enormous dosages. The present degree of knowledge indicates that when properly prescribed the side effects in no way compare with those from antidepressant medication. But there are some precautions involved with amino acid therapy. Particular care must be exercised when starting amino acid therapy in children and the elderly, and when starting amino acid therapy in anyone who has recently taken antidepressant medication of the MAO inhibitor class. Precursor therapy is not a therapy for self help, even though amino acids are readily available without prescription.

Since not all physicians utilize this treatment, or many of the other treatments described in this book, please refer to chapter 19, "Choosing a Doctor."

The doctor you choose may proceed, after taking a history,

by prescribing some amino acids based solely on experience, or the choice may be made to do laboratory tests on blood and urine samples to determine the level of amino acids in your body. The tests may be helpful in determining which amino acids are lacking and could help in the prescription of the amino acids.

The amino acids which have been most beneficial in the treatment of depression are l-tyrosine, l-phenylalanine and l-tryptophan. It is not the intention to give a formula for treatment, but only information about which amino acids have been found to be most helpful. When a condition as serious as depression is present, even though natural substances may be used for therapy, the treatment should be under the direction of a qualified physician.

Generally it is important to accompany the amino acid treatment with vitamin supplements, particularly B vitamins. Sometimes other amino acids are used, but at a lower dosage, in an attempt to prevent the development of any significant imbalance in the amino acid metabolism when one or two amino acids are being ingested in abnormally high quantities.

To be most effective, the amino acids must be taken at the proper time. In order to do their work they must be transported to the brain. The transport is slowed down if there are many other amino acids present competing for transportation. Therefore, most often, when using amino acids in singular form, they should be taken on as empty a stomach as possible, which usually means between meals. They should not be taken with protein food or drink such as milk. A small amount of insulin usually enhances transportation, so the amino acids may be taken with a small amount of fresh juice, which causes an insulin response and enhances transportation.

Although there are many reasons for the neurotransmitter defects, some of which are certainly genetic, the use of precursor therapy has been able to bridge the gap between the various causes to effect a beneficial response in many cases. This is a most promising form of natural therapy, which has been effective in cases where all else has failed. Precursor therapy is another therapeutic tool available to the physician to combat depression.

Suggested reading:

The Way Up from Down, Priscilla Slagle, M.D., Random House, 1987.

CHAPTER 17

The Psychotherapies

AT 3:00 A.M., the young woman was restless and feeling the hopelessness and sadness of her life. She was frightened by the overwhelming thoughts of suicide even as a small part of her was hanging on to the possibility that life could eventually be beautiful. This particular morning was a bad one, because her depression was getting worse. She had not been able to sleep more than a few hours during the night, and the thoughts of suicide obsessed her.

In a search for help, she went to the nearest hospital emergency clinic, where the admitting clerk pigeonholed her complaints neatly into a psychiatric classification. He called the psychiatric resident, who arrived awakening from sleep but eager to help. An assessment of the condition of the somewhat bedraggled, sad-faced, teary-eyed girl as being depressed was so obvious that expert medical training was not necessary for a diagnosis. The resident quickly asked, as if Freud himself were the questioner, "Why do you hate your father?"

The patient, surprised and thinking that the doctor had not really understood the pain she was experiencing, began to explain what she was doing at the hospital at 3:00 a.m. After listening to her complaints of sadness, hopelessness, suicidal fears, he repeated his question, "Why do you hate your father?" At this point the patient, who had never been aware of any hate for her father, began to feel that she was a participant in the Mad Hatter's tea party. She excused herself and went home, to try again the following day with another psychiatrist.

The evaluations of the psychotherapies are not so much whether they are good or bad, but whether this method is appropriate or inappropriate. Naturally, the skill and logic of the psychotherapist is also involved. The sleepy-eyed, eager resident psychiatrist was using a valid method of psychotherapy inappropriately. The same question about the patient's relationship with her father, when asked after an investigation into the patient's past relationships and at a time when she was able to consider the question, might have resulted in help for the patient. But the therapist would have to be well prepared with the facts obtained from previous interviews to suspect that a relationship of hate existed. He would also have to be reasonably certain that what he had learned about the patient confirmed his suspicions that the feeling of hate was relevant to the patient's complaint of depression. It may possibly be an interesting observation with no particular relevance to the depression and the complaints at hand.

Further, it would be necessary to pose the question when the patient indicated some receptiveness. In order to judge that type of timing, the therapist needs skill combined with knowledge of his patient's background. When all of these factors are analyzed, there is a possibility that the insight offered by such a piercing question could be therapeutic. Without this background, the unskilled therapist is only attempting to fit the patient into a preconceived and poorly conceived mold. Instead of a therapeutic response to this cliche, the patient left the clinic apprehensive and wondering about the relevance of psychiatry in general and the sanity of the psychiatrist in particular.

TREATMENTS FOR DEPRESSION

As I have mentioned, the patient, in attempting to get professional help for his problems, is confronted with numerous possibilities—medical, psychiatric and nutritional. When there are many choices, all attempting to solve the same problem, it is probable that there does not exist one perfect, right and complete answer for that problem. If there were such an all encompassing answer, there obviously would not be a need for so many methods.

And so it is with the treatment of depressions. Within the three general areas, whether the problem is physical or psychological, there are many schools of thought. The psychotherapies have one thing in common and that is the belief that the problem for which the patient seeks help has a psychological cause and, therefore, the treatment is directed towards dealing with the psychological problem. Within this framework the patient is confronted with a multitude of approaches, extending from nude group sessions to lying on a couch three times a week by himself and saying whatever comes into his head to an almost voiceless presence, who miraculously regains his voice at the end of each hour to indicate that the time is up. In psychotherapy, the patient has the choice of being treated in a group or by himself.

Group therapies, involving a few to very many people, also show considerable variation. In some groups the patients sit with the therapist and discuss their problems, thoughts, feelings, solutions and share with each other their experiences and suggestions. In such a group, recurrent mistakes and unhealthy attitudes are highlighted and possible solutions are discussed. Other groups have a different orientation and feel that a discussion leading to intellectual insight is not therapeutic. In these groups there is an attempt to have an experience which leads to a happy solution of the disordered feelings. These groups may encourage physical contact among group participants.

154

THE PSYCHOTHERAPIES

Some groups encourage outward signs of release—such as screaming.

Sometimes groups vary not only in their psychological orientation but also in the timing of the sessions. Some of the more conventional group therapies meet from one to three hours a week. Other groups differ by the marathon nature of the meetings, which may last two or three days around the clock. Other groups might be distinguished by something in common shared by the participants, such as group therapy with families, adolescents, schizophrenics, to mention a few. These groups are brought together by similar complaints and interests, but the method of therapy probably doesn't differ from the types already mentioned; namely, the conventional "let's talk it out" or "let's touch it, act it or scream it out" types of therapy.

There is one group type of therapy that I feel deserves special attention. This is transactional analysis, commonly known as TA. This type of therapy is explained in the popular book, *I'm OK, You're OK,* by Thomas A. Harris, M.D. As with many therapies there is a special language used in this treatment. Part of the strength of TA is that the language is derived from everyday terms and those terms maintain their everyday meanings. Common terms are "parent," "child," "authority," and patients are urged to examine themselves and their relationships in those terms, which represent the various forces within each of us. Transactional analysis attempts to understand any disorder in mood, behavior, or relationships as a change in the equilibrium between parent, child and authority. The subsequent establishment of an improved equilibrium among the three forces can then lead to a healthier mood, behavior or relationship. In TA the terms are easy to understand and apply. Within a few sessions an individual is able to begin to see himself and to identify problems when they arise. The advantage of this approach is that he continues to do his own transactional analysis on a day-to-day basis.

The individual psychotherapies. The individual psychothera-

155

pies may be divided into analytic and non-analytic. The analytic therapies are usually given the name of the school of thought that developed the theory behind the treatment. The grandfather and originator of it all is, of course, Sigmund Freud. Many of Freud's students differed with him in areas of theory and left the fold to develop their own theory, which then carried their name. So we are now faced with many different analytic schools of thought—Freudian, Jungian, Adlerian and others which followed.

Freud may be compared to the genius who discovered something new, like the wheel. He was innovative, brilliant and ingenious. The men who followed and started their own schools were also bright, but their perception may be compared to the people who saw the original wheel and said, "Gee, I think it would roll better if it were smooth"; "It could be more pleasing if it were decorated." In some instances the followers improved the discovery, in some instances they detracted, but they all utilized Freud's original discoveries, from which they launched their own work.

Freud, who incidentally looked upon analysis as a research tool and not as a therapeutic aid, had written that he thought the treatment of many psychiatric disorders eventually would be chemical in nature. He also did not hesitate to change his mind. He was forever thinking, originating and reviewing. He seemed satisfied that he had never reached the ultimate truth. Following his death, many of his disciples fossilized his memory and defiled what he had achieved, which was to grow and develop. They accepted and insisted on "Freudian analysis" as it was last practiced by Freud. This was an injustice to the memory of a great man.

It is interesting to speculate in what areas this genius might have moved if he had been able to continue to develop. Is it likely that he would have stayed with the forms of therapy in practice fifty years ago? From the rate of his growth and the frequency of change in his theories, the only thing one can say is that he would not have remained static. I am confident that Freud, if he were alive today, would have progressed far beyond the psychoanalytic methods he was employing at the time of his death.

I do not agree with the critic who proclaimed that "Psychoanalysis is dead but it doesn't have the good grace to be buried." But the analysts who persist in stubbornly holding to their old theories that are losing relevance in today's world are hastening their own demise, even though their therapeutic tool continues to have limited therapeutic value. In a conference several years ago, analysts attempted to define analytic therapy. About the only definition that they could agree on was that if the patient visited a doctor three days a week then analysis was being done.

Because of the many practical problems—such as the frequency of the visits and the fact that the cost is beyond the reach of many patients—there are very few psychiatrists practicing analytic therapy exclusively any more. Many psychiatrists practice an analytically-oriented type of psychotherapy. In this treatment the theories of the analytic school are used but the method varies. Instead of visiting the psychiatrist three times a week, the patient may only visit once. Instead of the familiar couch, there would probably be a face-to-face meeting. Instead of the therapist periodically mumbling and grunting to prove that he is really wide awake and alert while sitting behind the prone patient, he actually probes and leads the patient into various discussions in the problem areas. This is a valid form of treatment when applied to the proper conditions. The value of the treatment, however, relies as heavily on the skill of the therapist as it does on the condition being treated.

In general, I have been discussing in the individual therapies the type that is known as insightful therapy. The theory is that if you can understand the why of your problem and gain insight

157

into its causes, then you can do something about it. Sometimes it works. Insightful therapy usually necessitates digging into the past in order to gain an understanding of how past events have led to the present problems. I find that patients must be strong to undergo the type of psychotherapy that insists on taking them back into the past. Many people who are not that strong have a bad response to this type of psychotherapy as it may open "a can of worms."

Other psychotherapies may be classed as supportive or directive. These terms are self explanatory. In this type of treatment the condition is seen as a temporary one and, from knowledge of the patient's past experience, the physician knows that the problem will pass. As an example, take the case of Dennis, a young homosexual, who had been in a happy relationship with his lover for over two years. His background revealed that he was a survivor who had personal resources of intelligence and determination which had, in the past, always pulled him through troubled times.

When his lover left abruptly to live with someone else, Dennis was miserable, frightened, depressed. It was necessary to give him support by letting him know that there was someone with whom he could talk. While listening to him, it was important to point out, when he had calmed down and was able to comprehend, that he was not worthless and that he had overcome difficult problems in the past and would do so in this instance. With some patients it is enough just to have someone available when they need help. Others gain strength by the confidence they feel when talking with the therapist. I have often wondered, in considering the various psychotherapies, how much of the therapeutic value is related to the supportive nature of the relationship and how much is due to the insight towards which the work is directed. My feeling has always been that the benefit from most of the talking therapies is due to the supportive aspects of the relationship.

For Dennis it was not enough to be supportive. I also gave him a sense of direction. By having a general knowledge of his background, it was obvious that it would be important for him to finish college, since he was only a set of examinations and five weeks away from graduation. So, by reinforcing his goal, I was able to help him through some of the confusion that he was experiencing. It was also important to suggest that he take one step at a time and to live on a day-to-day basis until he felt better. My job was simply taking what looked like an insoluble problem for a frightened, insecure, depressed young man and placing his goals into a logical sequence of stages, each one capable of being solved.

Other than analysts who are trained in a particular school of analysis—which is the training in addition to the internship and residency which all psychiatrists go through—most psychiatrists do not belong to a particular school of thought. Most psychiatrists in their psychotherapy have borrowed from many schools and will call themselves eclectic. The eclectic psychiatrist is not bound to the pure psychiatric teachings of any one school. A large number of general psychiatrists now practice in this way.

There are, of course, many more therapies available. I've covered most of the common psychotherapies. An excellent book has been written by Thomas Kiernan called *Shrinks, Etc.—A Consumer's Guide to Psychotherapies*, published by the Dial Press. That well-written, much-needed book describes in detail the various schools of analysis as well as group and individual therapies. Anyone contemplating entering into psychotherapy will find a lot of information about what is available in the world of psychotherapy from that book.

CHAPTER 18

Convulsive Therapy

AFTER OTHER TYPES of treatment have failed—or because of the severity of the patient's depression or serious suicidal risk— I may suggest shock treatment. The man who developed this treatment should be given a medal. But the man who gave it its name should have been shot. Whenever I suggest shock treatment to a patient, sometimes it is hard to get the words out without feeling that I am conveying a picture from one of those Grade B movies, in which the horrified victim is dragged to a Frankenstein laboratory, held down by five drooling, slightly deformed and grinning assistants, while the doctor pulls the lever, causing the victim to jerk around the table in exaggerated convulsions.

I often think that this is the image that patients and their families have when the idea of convulsive therapy is mentioned. Quite frankly, it is often difficult to overcome the stigma of the word SHOCK, yet I have used the treatment successfully in my practice, as have untold numbers of other psychiatrists.

The method of administering the treatment has varied over the years. Before the use of certain drugs which relax the muscles, the main complication of shock treatment was broken bones. The sudden convulsion with strong muscles contracting resulted in some fractures. The necessity of being held or tied to prevent falling off the treatment table resulted in further fractures. Several years after the introduction of ECT, drugs were discovered which relax the muscles so that strong convulsions do not take place. In most centers this type of modified treatment with drugs is used.

The patient is given an intravenous injection of barbiturate which induces sleep. When sleep has been achieved, a muscle relaxant is given in the same vein. When the patient is fully relaxed, the electrical stimulus is applied. After the proper amounts of medication are given, the convulsion may be reduced to some rhythmical twitching of the toes. If too much muscle relaxant is given, the development of "goose flesh" and the enlargement of the pupils are signs that the proper electrical stimulus has been given. Oxygen is administered to the patient before the electrical stimulation and after the convulsion. The total time that the patient sleeps is usually less than five minutes. On awakening there is a confusion which may last for a few hours. The patient is usually groggy and it is best to encourage sleep for another 20 to 30 minutes.

Treatments are usually given three times a week for a total of six to ten treatments. Sometimes less than six treatments are effective; sometimes more are necessary. Frequency of treatment varies from several in one day to one treatment daily, but most practitioners use a three-times-a-week schedule. Some medical folklore suggests that three times a week was the chosen number because that was the number of times that orgasm was thought to occur in healthy individuals. It was further postulated that ECT was, in some way, a sexual substitute, thus accounting for its benefits. I know of no one who adheres to such an explanation today, but three treatments a week are the usual frequency because it has worked.

Sometimes a patient will feel that he is too old or too sick to have electroconvulsive treatment (ECT). About the only condition I know in which this treatment should definitely not be used is when the patient has a brain tumor. In the case of a brain tumor, there have been some deaths following ECT. These were due to the treatment and not to the anesthetic agents. A brain tumor obviously takes up space in the head, which has a limit on the space available because of the closed structure of the skull. Following shock treatment there may be a swelling of the tumor, which is enough to cause damage by pressure to some of the vital brain centers. There is no other condition that really prevents ECT, and so I have no reservations about using this treatment when it becomes necessary. Of course, there are many medical conditions in which the patient is so ill physically that the risk of danger from the anesthesia is far greater than the treatment itself. In those cases sober medical judgment must decide on the relative risks involved.

I have treated and seen many high-risk patients with serious heart problems, even pacemakers, and many elderly patients with generalized weakened conditions where ECT was, in my judgment and in the judgment of the consultants who were requested to see the patient, a life-saving procedure. The youngest patient I have seen treated with ECT was when I was clinical director of Gracie Square Hospital. That patient was under ten. The oldest? Near ninety. The most seriously ill patient I have treated was a woman in her mid-thirties. She had two artificial valves placed in her heart and several postoperative complications requiring further surgery. She remained in the intensive care unit for weeks, and, when she began to respond, she developed the idea that she was in a concentration camp and was being persecuted by the Nazis, who were poisoning her food. Naturally, she stopped eating, drinking and violently fought off all attempts to administer medication and intravenous feedings. Because of continued weight loss and ineffective medication, I advised, and the consultants agreed, that shock treatment was the only method that might salvage this patient, whose medical condition was rapidly deteriorating.

A team consisting of an anesthesiologist, cardiologist, myself and a well-trained ECT staff proceeded with the treatments. She had absolutely no complications and progressed as most patients do. She soon lost her fear of being poisoned and began to eat and take medication. She gained weight and, for the most part, became healthy again. She did not relapse into her psychotic state and left the hospital to resume her household duties. She did retain a few neurotic problems which had been present for years.

The development of convulsive therapy is a fairly typical story in science. An effective treatment was developed starting with the wrong premise. It was an observation of some clinicians that those people suffering with epilepsy never exhibited the symptoms of what we now call schizophrenia. The idea developed that the convulsions must in some way protect epileptics from schizophrenia. Therefore, by producing convulsions, schizophrenia could be cured. This idea was put to the test over a number of years in a number of ways. The first problem was to develop a method to produce a convulsion. Chemicals were injected and inhaled and were effective, but there was a disadvantage. In the earlier methods it was never known when the convulsion would occur. It was completely unpredictable. To be able to produce a convulsion at an exact time would be most desirable. For example, the patient needed to be observed during the convulsion or he might hurt himself. It is difficult to offer assistance if you don't know the exact time the convulsion will occur.

Finally, in the 1930s, Cerlitti and Bini, working in Rome, developed a method of applying electrical current to each side of the head for a brief period of time. In so doing they were able to produce a convulsion at a specified time; when the

163

current was applied the convulsion occurred. This is a great advantage over the guesswork of the previous methods.

Through the years it was observed repeatedly that the bizarre symptoms of schizophrenia did respond to convulsive therapy. Also it was confirmed that the original observation of epileptics not having schizophrenia was false. Epileptics do indeed have schizophrenia.

There have been several theories as to why ECT is effective (*Pharmacological Convulsive and other Somatic Treatments in Psychiatry*, Kalinowsky, Hippius, published by Greene & Stratton). The theories range from psychoanalytic explanations on how the patient wants to be punished to biochemical explanations on how the chemicals known as neurotransmitters are changed through electrical stimulation. While there may be no consensus as to why ECT works, most observers do admit that it does work.

As ECT was being used more and more, physicians observed that it was very effective in some of the depressive disorders. ECT is still a therapeutic option in some cases of depression and schizophrenia. The utilization of ECT has been greatly restricted and controlled in some states.

There are some side effects that the patient should know about. Following the first treatment, there may be a soreness of the muscles, especially in the jaw and neck. This occurs only after the first treatment and lasts up to 24 hours. Headache, nausea and vomiting are distressing side effects which occur sometimes. When they are present, it is usually attributed to the medication given prior to the treatment. Other medications can counteract these side effects, or a change in the pre-treatment medications may be necessary.

Memory loss, which does occur, is the most undesirable side effect. Of course, some patients welcome shock treatments because they think it will block out their memory of unpleasant events. But the memory loss is not the reason ECT is effective.

The loss of memory varies, depending mainly on the age of the patient and frequency of treatments.

The loss of memory is usually temporary. Within seven to ten days following the last treatment, most of the memory has returned. Some technical information may need to be relearned but this is done rapidly, requiring only a short review of the material. Simple things like people's names and telephone numbers may need review rather than spontaneously returning. The memory loss is progressive during the course of treatment, becoming a little worse with each treatment. With most people, after about the fourth treatment there is some carry-over in loss from day to day. Prior to that, the memory usually returns within a few hours.

The big exception to the transitory nature of memory loss is when ECT is given to people who already have some loss due to a disease of their brain, such as arteriosclerosis of the brain arteries. The memory loss in these conditions comes on quickly and severely and may be permanent. ECT has to be used with the greatest caution in someone showing signs of brain disease.

While several methods have been tried to overcome the memory loss—such as varying the type of electrical current given—the most recent and effective method is called unilateral ECT. Instead of applying electrical stimulation to both sides of the head, the stimulus is applied to only one side of the head. The brain has two sides: dominant and nondominant. The dominance can be determined fairly accurately by a number of simple questions, such as right-handedness or left-handedness, which foot is used to kick a ball, which eye is used to look through a hole in a piece of paper. If the right side of the body is used in these examples, then the left side of the brain is dominant and the right side is nondominant. There is a switch-over in the workings of the human brain; the left side controls the right side of the body and the right side controls the left side of the body. Having established right or left dominance, the nondominant side of the brain is given the electrical stimulus. This causes less memory impairment. Dominance can be deceptive and the physician must be aware of this. I have had patients who passed all the tests for right-side dominance, only to develop the usual memory loss when stimulated on the supposed nondominant right side. When the stimulation was switched to their left side, they responded, as would be expected, if the nondominant side were being stimulated. Patients who have unilateral treatment wake up without any memory loss. Many of these patients can be back in their offices within a few hours of treatment and functioning normally through the day as opposed to the confusion on the day of the bilateral treatment.

While unilateral treatment is effective, it usually requires a few more treatments than the conventional bilateral treatments. Because there is no memory loss, treatments may be given daily. This somewhat speeds up the recovery. When treatments are given in a hospital, the total hospital time might be shortened by giving unilateral treatments daily, even though treatments may be necessary after the patient is discharged. Combinations of bilateral and unilateral treatments may be used. Sometimes the treatments are alternated, depending on the response and the memory impairment.

Although there are some side effects, they are relatively rare. For example, one seldom sees a broken bone. A very small percentage of schizophrenic patients show increased symptoms under shock treatment. This always presents a difficult decision for the physician because, if the symptoms of schizophrenia are becoming worse, the treatment plan would be to continue ECT. If, however, the bizarre symptoms are due to the memory loss caused by the treatment, then treatment should be stopped at once. But I cannot remember any of my patients who were depressed who went into a deeper depression following the shock treatment. This adverse effect seems to occur in only a few schizophrenic patients undergoing ECT.

CONVULSIVE THERAPY

As I have indicated, the possible serious consequences of ECT are usually due to the medications given for anesthesia and muscle relaxation. A small number of patients will have serious reactions to these drugs and some deaths have resulted. This situation is rare. I want to emphasize that this is only a probability. Saying that there is a danger doesn't convey the probability that the danger will happen. For example, there is a danger in driving an automobile down Fifth Avenue in New York City during the rush hour. But millions of people have made this drive without the slightest mishap. In the same way, while there is a possibility of serious consequences with medication prior to treatment, the probability is very low.

The patient and his family should know what to expect during the treatment. When improvement does take place, there are certain signs to look for. I always feel that even a short period of minutes or hours of relief following the first treatment is a good sign. Usually after each treatment there is a progressively longer period of relief, but it is not until the third or fourth treatment that the relief of the symptoms lasts from one day to the next.

A few treatments are usually continued past the point of the first response; for example, if, after the fourth treatment the response is lasting from one day to the next and the symptoms and signs of depression are clearing up, probably the treatments would stop somewhere after the sixth. Sometimes the last few treatments are given at longer intervals than every other day.

If the treatments are given to a patient who is not hospitalized, the patient should be accompanied to and from the treatment. Because of a possible memory loss, the patient should be advised not to drive and he should be looked after by someone. Also, the patient should have nothing to eat or drink for several hours prior to the treatment. Treatments are usually given in the morning, but they can be given later in the day, providing several hours have elapsed since eating or drinking.

167

TREATMENTS FOR DEPRESSION

Families and patients should be forewarned about the possible memory loss and other changes during the course of the treatment so they can be prepared to deal with it.

A legitimate complaint against ECT is that sometimes the good effects don't last. This is true in some cases. But I am more concerned about the small percentage of cases that do not respond at all. For those cases where there is a response, even if the response doesn't last, there is a modification of technique that has been responsible for helping many people. In those cases, a treatment is given on a regular basis, anywhere from once a week at the beginning to once every four to six weeks on an indefinite schedule. This type of program—called maintenance ECT—is very effective where electroconvulsive treatment works but doesn't last.

ECT is an effective therapeutic tool that has not been replaced completely by other methods. When used properly, it is safe and effective in a large number of cases. The response is relatively rapid, which makes it particularly desirable for those people who are depressed, absolutely hopeless and feel that they cannot stand the pain of depression any longer.

PART 5

Finding Help

CHAPTER 19

Choosing a Doctor

WHEN YOU'RE DEPRESSED, the last thing you want to do is exert energy in shopping for a doctor. But a few thoughtful hours in thinking through the problem may pay off in a more rapid return to health. The first question is whether or not a doctor is necessary. Some of the factors to consider: 1) The severity of the depression; 2) The duration of the depression; 3) The symptoms of the depression (for example, suicidal thoughts and loss of appetite); 4) Past experience with the depression.

If a person is experiencing a mild depression and has no history of mental illness, then professional help may not be necessary. It is quite natural to be depressed for a short period. Usually such depressions run their course in a few weeks or days. If the person is experiencing intense sadness with possible thoughts of suicide, and there is no sign of relief, then professional guidance is certainly warranted.

If there is some hesitation about going to a doctor, perhaps because of a previous unpleasant experience, then family members should volunteer their advice. When there is a clear-cut psychological cause for the depression—and admittedly this is

171

often difficult for the layman to determine—the treatment should be oriented to psychotherapy. The wife whose husband has left her, the businessman whose business has failed, the student who has run out of money for continuing his studies are some of the examples that are mostly psychological. The danger is that when depression is suspected, a cause can usually be found that will fit neatly into some psychological niche. If there are recurrent depressions that must be continually explained, then the psychological cause is probably less significant and a medical cause should be sought.

Many of my patients who have experienced severe, repeated depressions have said, "I have always felt that there is something wrong with my body chemistry." I have learned to trust the patients' intuitive sense about this reaction and approached their problem from a purely medical aspect.

Of course, the psychotherapies vary just as much as the medical approaches do. Therefore, it might be helpful to involve friends or neighbors who have any knowledge in this area. In the larger cities there is often a branch of the American Psychiatric Association which maintains a list of psychiatrists who specialize in the various psychiatric methods. Usually the name of a physician who is interested in psychotherapy or drug therapy, convulsive therapy, etc., is available from the APA offices or the local medical society.

Local medical societies may have a listing of their member physicians who specialize in nutritional medicine and/or orthomolecular psychiatry. If your local association does not have any referrals some of the professional organizations whose members are involved with nutritional medicine may be contacted. One organization is The Huxley Institute for Biosocial Research, of Boca Raton, Florida, whose address and telephone numbers are given on page 45.

The Huxley Institute is an affiliation of professional and lay organizations who have had as their primary interest through the years, the use of nutrient therapy for a variety of illnesses, including nervous disorders. At the present time the Academy of Orthomolecular Medicine, formerly the Academy of Ortho- molecular Psychiatry, the Orthomolecular Medical Society and the American Schizophrenia Association are divisions of The Huxley Institute. The Huxley Institute sponsors several seminars on topics pertinent to Nutritional Medicine. These seminars are held in different locations throughout the year. They also have an extensive collection, available for purchase, of books, arti- cles, pamphlets and audio tapes relevant to nutritional topics.

After you have located a physician, you should confirm by phone that the doctor or psychotherapist actually uses the ther- apy which you are seeking. For example, if it has been deter- mined that medication and psychotherapy are needed, a few simple questions will confirm that you are making an appoint- ment with the right professional. You might ask, "Do you do psychotherapy, doctor?" "Do you use medication if it is necessary?" "Do you approve of megavitamin therapy?" etc. Some very responsible psychiatrists will not use medication of any kind and will tell you. Knowing your options beforehand will save a great deal of time, money and disappointment. If you suspect that you may have hypoglycemia, or low blood sugar, you should mention this to the doctor and inquire whether or not a glucose tolerance test will be necessary.

Even if you have preconceived ideas about a specific treat- ment, you must give the doctor time to work on your case. In the case of megavitamin therapy, as we have commented, it takes time for your body to adjust to a new diet and the addition of food supplements. Also remember medication takes time and psychotherapy takes time. Be patient, don't try to rush results. It can't be done. The therapy you choose doesn't necessarily have to make you feel good immediately, but it should make sense. Do not expect an instant improvement every time you see the therapist. Therapy, whether it is medical, psychological

173

or nutritional, must be one with which you feel comfortable. If the therapy seems bizarre and a waste of time, you should question the doctor about it. If you are convinced that the treatment is wrong for you, it will only impede your recovery. If you think it might work, give it a chance. Rarely does anyone become depressed overnight. Rarely does anyone lose a depression overnight.

With the counsel of family and friends, the family doctor, the agencies that I mention in this book, or the family minister, priest or rabbi, a suitable psychotherapist can usually be found. With all of the professional help that is available, no one should ever stay depressed.

As I have stated, there are professional and non-professional sources of help in almost every community. They have experience with all types of depression, so your case is not unique. With a little help on your part, they can steer you into the right direction. To restate my thesis: You need not stay depressed. Help is on the way.

CHAPTER 20

What Help Is Available

HAVING DECIDED THAT help is necessary to treat the depression, the patient is then faced with the problem: "What kind of help do I need?" An optimist might not have any problem, but the depressed person and his worried family are anxious to determine their options. To them the prospects are not too exciting, because they don't know where to turn.

In small communities, the choice is limited. They obviously do not have the agencies, therapists and physicians that are available in large metropolitan areas. Perhaps an explanation of some of the help that is available in the larger cities will take some confusion out of making a selection.

Self-Help Groups. These groups are usually made up of people who have experienced various problems of a psychiatric nature, therefore, they are eager to help. Most of the groups ask for small contributions from people who attend the meetings. The meetings are led by one of the members and a physician may or may not be present. In deciding whether or not to attend such meetings, it is best to sit in on several sessions in order to observe what happens. The content of the meeting must make sense and must be pertinent to the problems you have.

Also, it is necessary to be aware that groups have their own personalities just like people. Even though what is said might make sense, you might not like the group. In that case, I advise my patients to try another group with similar intentions. Some of these are:

1) *Recovery, Inc.* This non-profit organization has meetings in most of the major cities in the U.S. There are often several groups meeting in the same city. The meetings are conducted by one of the members, who follows the guidelines set forth in *Mental Health Through Will Training* by the late Abraham A. Low, M.D. Participation is voluntary and open to anyone 18 years of age or older. Recovery, Inc. does not work to displace the physician's role in the care of the patient, but it is not necessary to have a physician in order to attend these meetings.

I have referred many patients to Recovery, Inc. Among the many advantages are: 1) There is a consistency in the method and in the meetings, no matter where the meeting is held. 2) The method makes sense. By following the Recovery method, a person is more able to cope with some devastating aspects of anxieties and depressions. 3) The group is supportive and not destructive in its discussions. 4) One to several meetings a week may be attended. 5) Cost is very low since there is no fee. A small contribution is requested. The only other cost is the purchase of the above-named book.

The listing for most chapters of Recovery, Inc. may be found in the white pages of the local phone book. If no listing is found the National Headquarters may be contacted by phone or mail to find the nearest meeting. The headquarters also provides for a contribution of $2 a national directory of all chapters.

Recovery, Inc.
802 N. Dearborn
Chicago, IL 60610
312-337-5661

2) *Emotional Health Anonymous.* This organization has several chapters in Southern California and over the past several years chapters have been added in other sections of the country. Whenever possible they are listed in the local phone directory, but if there is no listing information may be obtained by contacting:

Emotional Health Anonymous
2420 San Gabriel Boulevard
Rosemeade, California 91770
818-573-5482

This organization is comparatively small and is welcoming the formation of meetings in all sections of the country.

3) *Help Lines—Suicide Prevention.* Several metropolitan areas have a manned, 24-hour telephone service. For those people who feel depressed, perhaps suicidal, and don't know where to turn, a simple telephone call to the Suicide Prevention Center (listed in the phone book) may be the beginning stage of obtaining significant help. For one thing it puts you in immediate personal contact with a sympathetic person.

Non-Physician Therapists. Psychotherapy is not limited to physicians. Many fine therapists have never been inside a medical school. Psychologists, social workers, clergymen are all trained to help the desperate person. Sometimes psychiatrists object to the practice of psychotherapy by others, since they feel that the depression may have a medical origin and a trained psychiatrist with a medical degree will be better qualified to recognize a disease.

My own experience with nonmedical therapists has been very good. I find that they are usually very much aware of possible medical causes of illness and frequently suggest that patients have a medical examination. Quite often they work closely with a physician, who is available for consultation for medical prob-

177

lems. One cannot determine the competency of an individual based on his degrees. But the irony of the value of medical vs. nonmedical psychotherapists becomes more pronounced when one realizes how little attention is paid to the patient's medical condition by some psychiatrists who have medical degrees.

The M.D. Therapist. The most confusion probably exists in the supermarket of M.D. therapists. In trying to unravel the multitude of possibilities, you might think of two major approaches to the therapy of depression by the psychiatrists. One major approach represents the physical treatments, the other the psychological treatments. The obvious assumption of the psychological approach is that there is a psychological problem at the root of the depression and that, by some form of talk therapy or other types of communication, the depression will disappear or at least improve.

As I have stated throughout this book, there are many psychological theories of depression and there are many modifications of the treatment techniques. Some psychological theories hold that the base of the depression is the loss of something; other theories concentrate on the emotion of anger, which is presumed to be turned inwards towards oneself. The techniques vary widely from the classical Freudian analysis, where the patient lies on a couch three to five times a week saying anything that comes into his head, to the various types of group therapies that I have discussed. Whatever the theory of depression or whatever the technique of treatment, the basic assumption is that the disorder that results in the disease of depression is psychological.

Opposed to this assumption is the group that feels depression is a medical problem. The obvious approach of this group is to treat the medical condition. The problem here is that, in most cases, the medical cause of depression has not been found. Some of the causes are known, but, frankly, they are not the common ones seen by the psychiatrist nowadays. For example,

178

it is known that thyroid pathology may result in depression. But it is usually the family physician who finds the thyroid disease before the patient consults a psychiatrist. As I mentioned earlier, pellagra, a niacin deficiency disease, causes depression. It is believed to be relatively rare today, yet some physicians believe that depressed people suffer from a sub-clinical form of pellagra. In other words, they do not have the usual symptoms that would cause many physicians to recognize that they have pellagra, yet, because of a niacin deficiency, they have some of the symptoms.

Fortunately, some of the medical treatments have been found before the medical causes are known. The most widely used medical treatments for depression are medication and less frequently electro convulsive treatments. Although much is known about these two forms of treatment and how they affect the chemistry of the body, there is not yet a clear understanding of the biochemistry of depression, particularly the role of the chemicals that transmit the impulses from one nerve cell to another.

Many research scientists are looking at these chemicals for their involvement in many psychiatric disorders. But, for the most part, the medical or biochemical causes of depression are as yet undefined. But, as I have demonstrated in many case histories, the most neglected medical treatment for depression is nutritional therapy and especially the treatment of hypoglycemia with vitamins and diet.

Therefore, the treatment of depression is not a simple medical vs. psychological choice. There are many types of depression and each individual has his own variation on the depression he is experiencing. It is for this reason that the therapist, even though he may be skilled in one particular school of thought, must keep a broad perspective in order to offer the most help to his patients.

179

INDEX

181

Index

Beverages. *See* Alcohol; Caffeine; Liquids
Biochemical abnormality, 42–43, 134–135, 172, 179
Birth defects, 129
Blood sugar. *See* Hypoglycemia
Blood tests, 117–118
Blurred vision, 58, 133
The Book of Health, 22
Bowel habits, 7, 110
Brain, 40–41, 49, 165
  see also Neurotransmitters
Brain tumor, 162
Bread, whole-grain, 62
Breathing problems, 58
Bruises, 128
Bunney, W. E., Jr., 141
Butler, Dr. Thorne, 128

Cade, Dr. John F. J., 137
Caffeine, 59, 63
Calories, 61, 64, 96
Candidiasis. *See* Yeast infections
Caprylic acid, 113
Carbohydrates, 48, 58, 112
  see also Low-carbohydrate diet; Sugar
Carbonated water, 61
Carroll, Sheila, 123
Case illustrations
  child hypoglycemic, 47–48
  convulsive therapy, 162–163
  diversity of depression, 4–5
  hypoglycemia, successful treatments, 75–89
  lithium use, 137–139
  medications for depression, 130–132
  misapplied psychotherapy, 152–153
  suicide, 22–23, 25, 28
The CFIDS Association, Inc., 105–106
CFS. *See* Chronic Fatigue Syndrome
Cheese, 96, 113
Cherry, Rona and Laurence, 136
Children
  amino acid therapy precautions, 149
  hyperactivity, 46, 47–49
  overmedication of, 128–129
Chlordiazepoxide, 125, 129

Cholesterol, 61
Chronic Fatigue Syndrome (CFS), 104–106
Clark, Dr. Randolph Lee, 22
Clergymen, 177
Coffee, decaffeinated, 61
  see also Caffeine
Cold sweats, 57
Compazine, 124
Concentration loss, 58
Confusion, mental, 31, 57
  effect of diet on, 70
Convenience foods, 39–40
Convulsions, 58
Convulsive therapy, 4, 160–168, 179
  bilateral and unilateral, 165–166
  contraindictions, 162
  history, 163–164
  maintenance, 168
" 'Cooling It' on Tranquilizers," 129
Cott, Dr. Allan, 46
Cough, 110
Cousins, Norman, 17
Crying spells, 58
Cumley, Dr. Russell W., 22

Dairy products, 62, 64
Dalmane, 130
Davis, Adelle, 127–128
Delayed reactions, food, 116–117
Dementia, 144
Depression
  amino acids for, 145–151
  available help, 175–179
  breaks in, 19–20
  convulsive therapy for, 160–168
  diagnosis of, 30–32
  as a disease, 3, 10, 21, 30
  family's view of, 3–4, 11–21
  feelings associated with, 3, 5–6, 8–10, 17, 31–32
  food sensitivities and, 116–117
  healing period, 19
  hypoglycemia and, 56, 57, 58, 65, 67, 92
  kinds and degrees of, 13–14
  lithium for, 136–144

182

Index

medical treatment for, 15–16, 171–174

medication for, 123–135

nutrition and, 39–46, 144

patient's view of, 3, 8–10, 19–20

physical signs of, 7, 9

physical vs. psychological causes of, 33–34, 178

physician's view of, 15–16, 30–35

prevalence of, 3

psychotherapies, 152–159

recovery, ups and downs in, 20

suicide and, 8, 12, 23, 26–29

treatments, 123–167, 179

typical cases, 4–5

viruses and, 101–106

yeast infections and, 107–115

Diabetes, 191–92, 93

Diagnosis

of depression, 30–32

of food sensitivities, 117–118

of hypoglycemia, 52–55, 56, 58, 94

Diet and nutrition

appetite change, 7, 9

drug-related deficiencies, 126–128

food sensitivities, 116–119

for hypoglycemia, 48, 59–74

importance of, 16

neurotransmitters and, 40

nutritional therapy, 39–46, 144

yeast infection treatment, 112–113

see also Megavitamin therapy

Digestive disturbances, 7, 57, 105, 110

yeast infection-related, 109–110, 113–114

Directive psychotherapy, 158–159

Disease, depression as, 3, 10, 21, 30

Dizziness, 51, 57, 65

Doctors. See Physician

The Doctor's Book of Vitamin Therapy, 126

Doriden, 126

Dr. Atkins' Diet Revolution, 124

Drowsiness, 57

Drug abuse, 27, 46, 123–130

Drugs. See Medication

"Drug Therapy of Depression—Amitriptyline, Perphenazine, and

Their Combination in Different Syndromes," 132

ECT. See Convulsive therapy

Eggs, 62

Elavil, 124

Elderly

amino acid therapy precautions, 149

suicides, 23

Electroconvulsive treatment (ECT). See Convulsive therapy

Emotional Health Anonymous, 177

Emotional strength, 74

Endocrine system, 92

Enriched white flour, 59, 63, 112

Epilepsy, 163, 164

Epstein-Barr virus, 101, 102–104, 105

Equanil, 125, 129

Exercise, 95, 96, 104

Exhaustion. See Fatigue

Fainting, 51, 56, 57

Family

attitude of, 16

help from, 18–21

interpreting suicide signs, 24

as part of recovery plan, 14–15

relations with depressed relative, 12–13

suicide history, 24, 25, 27

view of depressed relative, 3–4, 11–21

Farley, Dr. Otis R., 125

Fatigue

Chronic Fatigue Syndrome, 104–106

depression and, 32, 103

hypoglycemia and, 49, 56, 57, 64, 73, 92

yeast infection and, 110

FDA. See Food and Drug Administration

FDA Consumer, 128–129

Fears. See Anxiety; Phobias

Feldzamen, Dr. A. N., 126

Fernstrom, John, 40

Fetus, 129

Fever, low-grade, 105

Index

184

Index

additions to, 70–71
adjustment problems, 65–66
amount of food, 59, 63
avoidance foods, 63
cheating on, 64–65, 92–93
and exercise, 95, 96
frequency of snacks, 59, 63–64, 77, 94
improvement and, 73–74
individual adjustments, 60
maintenance program, 70–74
new food additions to, 72–73
for psychiatric stabilization, 124
and psychotherapy initiation, 68–69
questions and answers, 90–97
and smoking, 94–95
stages of, 65–70
successful case histories, 75–89
and surgery, 97
treatment program, 61–70
up/down days, 66–67
and vegetarianism, 95–96

IgG. *See* Immunoglobulin G
Immune system, 104, 105, 111–112
tranquilizers' effects on, 125, 126
Immunodiagnostic Laboratory of San Leandro, California, 111
Immunoglobulin G (IgG), 117–118
Immuno-Nutritional Clinical Laboratory, 118
I'm OK, You're OK, 155
Impotence, 58
Incoordination, 58
Indecisiveness, 57
Infectious mononucleosis, 101–102
see also Epstein-Barr virus
Insightful therapy, 157–158
Insomnia. *See* Sleep disturbances
Insulin, 50, 124, 150
Intravenous fluids, 97
Iron supplement, 76
Irritability, 32, 56, 57, 64

Jacobson, Michael, 39
Johnson, M., 132

Journal of the American Medical Association, 58
The Journal of Orthomolecular Psychiatry, 107
Junk foods, 64, 96

Keeping Healthy in a Polluted World, 128
Kiernan, Thomas, 159
Kimbell, I., 132
"Kissing disease." *See* Infectious mononucleosis

Labels, food product, 63
Lacto-ova-vegetarians, 95
Lancet, 125
Learning disorders, 46
Leg cramps, 58
Lethargy, 41
Let's Eat Right to Keep Fit, 127
Let's Get Well, 127
L-glutamine, 49
Librium, 124, 125, 129, 130, 132
Liquid protein, 64, 96
Liquids, 61
Lithium, 4, 136–144
side effects, 143
"Lithium in Depression and Mania: a Double-Blind Behavioral and Chemical Study," 141
"Lithium Salts in the Treatment of Psychotic Excitement," 137
Loss, depression following, 34
Low, Dr. Abraham A., 176
Low blood sugar. *See* Hypoglycemia
Low-carbohydrate diet, 43, 48, 59
avoidance foods, 63
different definitions, 60
see also Hypoglycemic diet
L-phenylalanine, 150
LSD, 27
L-tryptophan, 145–146, 150
L-tyrosine, 150

Manganese, 76, 77
Manic-depressives, 135–140

185

Index

MAO inhibitors. *See* Monoamine oxidase inhibitors
Massachusetts Institute of Technology, 40–41
Meats, 61, 64, 95
Medication, 4, 123–135, 173, 179
  and convulsive therapy, 161, 167
  for yeast infection, 113–114
  see also Drug abuse; specific types
Megavitamin therapy, 4, 17, 41–42, 45, 46, 173, 179
  case history successes, 76–89
  defined, 42
  and medications, 133
  see also Orthomolecular psychiatry
Megavitamin Therapy, 16–17
Memory, selective, 10
Memory loss, 164–166, 167, 168
Menstrual disturbances, 133
Mental confusion. *See* Confusion, mental
Mental Health Through Will Training, 176
Meprobamate, 124, 125, 129
Migraine headaches, 107
Milk, 62
Miltown, 125, 129
Minerals, 43
Mintz, Dr. Ronald, 25
The Missing Diagnosis, 108
Mold, 113
Monoamine oxidase (MAO) inhibitors, 133–134, 149
Moniliasis. *See* Yeast infections
Mood
  drugs altering, 123–124
  food sensitivities and, 116–119
  see also Depression; specific feelings
Morella, Joseph J., 124–125
Morrison, Margaret, 129
Mouth dryness, 133
Murphy, D. L., 141
Murray, Frank, 16–17
Muscle pains, 57, 103, 105
Muscle relaxants, 161, 167
Muscle soreness, 164
Mushrooms, 113

National Institutes of Mental Health Clinical Center, 141
"Natural sweeteners," 63, 91
Nausea, 65, 164
Nerve cells, 146–148
Nervousness, 32, 57
Neurodermatitis, 58
Neurons, 40, 41
Neurotransmitters, 40, 41, 134, 150–151, 164
  function, 146–148
New Age Nutrition, 124–125
New York Times, The, 105
Niacin. *See* Vitamin B3
Niacinamide, 48
Night terrors/nightmares, 58
Numbness, 57
Nutrient therapy. *See* Megavitamin therapy
Nutritional deficiency. *See* Diet and nutrition; Vitamin deficiencies
"Nutritional Side Effects of Drugs," 126–127
Nuts, 61, 64, 96
Nystatin, 113, 114

Oral contraceptives, 126, 144
Orthomolecular Medical Society, 173
Orthomolecular psychiatry, 4, 42–45, 173
  books and tapes source, 45
  defined, 42
  see also Megavitamin therapy
"Orthomolecular Psychiatry," 42
Orthomolecular Psychiatry, Treatment of Schizophrenia, 43
Osmond, Dr. Humphry, 42, 45
Overall, J. E., 132

Pantothenic acid, 48, 76, 127, 144
Pasta, 61–62
Past events, focus on, 10
Pau d'arco (tea), 114
Pauling, Dr. Linus, 42, 43
Pellagra, 17, 144, 178
Pennington, V., 132
Personal hygiene, 9

Index

187

Index

Index